# BRUGE
# AND A

## *in your pocket*

Travel Publications

MAIN CONTRIBUTOR: RUSSELL CHAMBERLIN

PHOTOGRAPH CREDITS
**Photos supplied by The Travel Library:**
106; Stuart Black front cover, 16, 32, 56, 58, 88, 91, 92,
93; Andrew Cowin back cover, title page, 4, 8, 10, 12, 18,
26, 28, 30, 31, 35, 36, 37, 38, 40, 41, 42, 43. 44, 46, 48, 49,
54, 59, 62, 63, 64(t,b), 65, 66, 69, 70, 71, 73, 74, 76, 78,
79, 80, 84, 86, 90, 95, 99, 100, 103, 107(t,b), 108, 113,
116, 119, 121, 123, 125; Freelance Pictures 51; R
Richardson 39; Peter Terry 60, 97.
**Other photos:**
Bridgeman Art Library, London/New York 23, 25, 68;
Giraudon/Bridgeman Art Library, London/New York
82; Tourism Flanders-Brussels 52, 53(t,b).

*Front cover: tranquil canal, Bruges; back cover: statue of
Silvius Brabo, Grote Markt, Antwerp; title page: detail of
guild house, Ghent.*

MANUFACTURE FRANÇAISE DES PNEUMATIQUES MICHELIN

Place des Carmes-Déchaux – 63000 Clermont-Ferrand (France)

© Michelin et Cie. Propriétaires-Éditeurs 1999

Dépôt légal Mars 99 – ISBN 2-06-652801-3 – ISSN 1272-1689

No part of this publication may be reproduced in any form

without the prior permission of the publisher.

Printed in Spain 01-01/2

**MICHELIN TRAVEL PUBLICATIONS**
Michelin Tyre plc
The Edward Hyde Building
38 Clarendon Road
WATFORD Herts WD1 1SX - UK
☎ (01923) 415000
www.michelin-travel.com

**MICHELIN TRAVEL PUBLICATIONS**
Michelin North America
One Parkway South
GREENVILLE, SC 29615
☎ 1-800 423-0485
www.michelin-travel.com

# CONTENTS

## INTRODUCTION

As with most countries today, tourism is a major industry in Belgium, and the government, realising the priceless assets of Antwerp, Bruges and Ghent, has begun marketing them together as 'cities of art'. And not without good reason, for these cities are like a story-book of their rich historic past, their streets reveal their heritage, their museums and galleries display their art and culture.

*The statue of Silvius Brabo hurls a hand across Grote Markt, surrounded by 16C Flemish guild houses.*

Few, if any, European cities today are as perfectly preserved as Bruges, which surely ranks as one of the most picturesque – indeed, is almost *too* perfect for some. To wander through its streets is like stepping back in time, its medieval buildings ironically saved by the city's economic decline – for centuries there was not the money to replace buildings or to modernise. Ghent has retained its areas of historical and artistic interest, but is altogether less of a museum piece and more of a vibrant, evolving city. The huge port of Antwerp, world centre for the diamond trade, also has its story to tell and historic quarters to explore. With its 43 museums and galleries, its magnificent churches and numerous historic buildings, Antwerp is more than qualified to be one of Flanders' 'cities of art'.

While it is true that these three cities have a concentration of art surpassed by few in Europe, and have much in common, they also have strong individual identities. Bruges is a compact jewel, set around its historic central square. A reasonably energetic person could explore it in a couple of days. Ghent is much larger, has no one centre and a complex of waterways created by the three rivers. Antwerp, although the largest of the three, is relatively easy to get to know, for its historic centre is marked out by the river.

Each city is ideal for a weekend break, with a wealth of attractions, art and history to satisfy even the most demanding of visitors, yet also compact enough for visitors to feel they have got to know the city in a few days. And if they should have more time to spare, for a real contrast there are the peaceful Polders and coastline to explore.

## GEOGRAPHY

Geographically, Belgium is a land of contrast and varied landscapes. In the south-east towards the Ardennes it is undulating, heavily wooded in places, the rivers moving swiftly between high banks. In Flanders the land is totally flat, the rivers broad and slow. Two millennia ago the whole of this region would have been marshy, with innumerable lakes and rivers. The boast of the Dutch that 'God made the sea but we made the land!' could equally be applied to Flanders. An illustration of this is the creation of **polders**. The plain, having been reclaimed through drainage canals, is protected by heaped-up dykes, with the canals used as lines of communication – an excellent example of human ingenuity turning natural obstacles into advantages.

Rivers and canals are the key to Flanders. The great river Scheldt, rising in France where it is known as the Escaut, runs almost due north to Ghent. There it is joined by the rivers Leie and Lieve before it takes a turn to the north-east onward to Antwerp. The river created Antwerp, transforming an inland city some 70km (40 miles) from the sea into Europe's second-largest port. Napoleon called the city 'a pistol aimed at England'. In the closing months of the Second World War, Adolf

**Map of the Flanders Region**

Hitler, in a desperate attempt to check the Allied advance, sent his tanks crashing through the Ardennes aiming for Antwerp; while its capture would not have altered the eventual outcome of the war, it would certainly have extended its duration. Similarly, it was a waterway, the river Zwin, that brought wealth to Bruges, until it silted up. Ghent, although without a natural link to the sea, was not to be outdone, and in the 14C dug a canal connecting it to the North Sea near Bruges. A more direct canal to Terneuzen, on the mouth of the Scheldt, has been successively widened since the 19C and is now a major industrial artery.

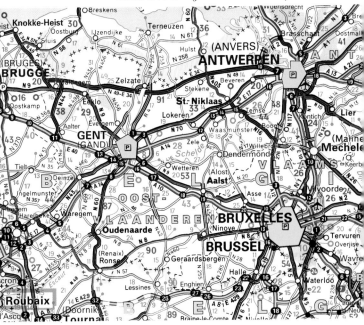

## HISTORY

Throughout history, Flanders has flickered into and out of legal existence in a bewildering manner. Sometimes it has existed as a separate state, sometimes it was totally subsumed into another, and currently it is in uneasy equipoise with Wallonia, its French-speaking neighbour.

*Reflections on the still, peaceful polders at dusk; a relaxing excursion from the bustling cities.*

## Early Beginnings

Some two thousand years ago the area which roughly corresponds with present-day Belgium was occupied by the **Belgae**, a Celtic warrior tribe. They were conquered by the **Romans**, under Julius Caesar around 57 BC, and the settlement of Ghent dates from this period. No sooner did the Romans withdraw from the area, than the **Franks** moved in.

In 498 the Frankish **King Clovis** was converted to Christianity, which gradually spread northwards, with Ghent being one of the last settlements to be converted from paganism, and the region attained a degree of unity. Political unity was not achieved until 768, when **Charlemagne** was crowned King of the Franks and established his kingdom. His empire expanded in Europe and in 800 he became the first Holy Roman Emperor.

There was not long to enjoy this attempt at European unity, however, which ended with the death of the great Emperor Charlemagne. At the Treaty of Verdun, in 843, his three grandsons partitioned his empire of Francia into three sections: West Francia (later France), East Francia (later Germany) and a middle section known as Lotharingia, named after Lothair who inherited the title, but not the power, of emperor. The line of division between West and East Francia was the Scheldt. Ironically, France inherited the predominantly Flemish-speaking north-west.

After the break-up of Charlemagne's empire, local lords began to appear. In the north-east, in the mid-11C emerged the first **Counts of Flanders**. Technically, they were vassals of the French kings and, although frequently acting as lords in their own right, they and the nobles of the towns were Francophile, unlike the body of the population, who saw the advantages of allegiance with England. Conflict between the Francophile counts and nobles and the Flemish merchants and workers was inevitable.

Despite their relatively recent foundation, the cities of Flanders grew wealthy with astonishing speed. They had easy access to one of the most coveted products of the Middle Ages – the wool from England, just a few miles away across the North Sea. The wool was turned into cloth which was sold around the civilised world, and the cloth towns of Bruges, Ghent and Ypres flourished.

*The statue of the Battle of the Golden Spurs boldly confirms the victories of Flemish workers over French nobility.*

The Flemish developed a highly disciplined workforce, organised in guilds. In almost every Flemish city today, the guild houses in which these guilds administered their affairs are an important architectural heritage. The stability and importance of the guilds are indicated by the fact that one of them in Ghent dates back as far as 1200.

As the cloth towns prospered, so the conflict between the Francophile nobles and the Flemish workers increased. Angered by the suppression of the guilds and the taxation imposed by the French-appointed governor, in May 1302 an army of workers from Bruges revolted, led by Pieter de Coninck and Jan Breydel, killing anyone they thought to be French. On 11 July 1302, near Kortrijk, the Flemish workers defeated an army of French nobles so soundly that it became known as the **Battle of the Golden Spurs**, from the 700 spurs collected from the bodies of the slain. Despite such resistance, French influence increased inexorably.

So vital was the English connection that in 1338, at the beginning of the long-drawn-out war between England and France, Jan van Artevelde, a merchant of Ghent, persuaded the Flemish cities to make an alliance with Edward III of England and so protect the supply of wool.

## Burgundian Flanders

The third section of Charlemagne's empire, Lotharingia, developed into the Duchy of Burgundy. Over the centuries this would expand and contract, sometimes stretching far south into Italy, sometimes far north to the North Sea. The immensely wealthy dukes of Burgundy were frequently more powerful than their supposed suzerain, the king of France, and had no hesitation in allying themselves with his enemies, in particular the English during the Hundred Years War.

In 1384 **Philip the Good**, Duke of Burgundy, married the daughter of Louis de Mael, Count of Flanders, and Flanders became part of the Dukedom of Burgundy. Philip the Good became Count of Flanders himself in 1419, gradually drawing most of Belgium, Holland and Luxembourg into his domain. Flanders lost its identity, but in return entered its **Golden Age**, for the dukes were not only wealthy but highly cultured, and noted for the splendour of their courts and their patronage of artists such as van Eyck and Memling. They moved their capital around the dukedom as they pleased, Dijon, Lille, Bruges and Brussels all serving as a capital at one time or another, so further blurring the distinction between Flanders and France.

Bruges, in particular, benefited from Burgundian rule. In 1430 Duke Philip the Good created, in Bruges, one of the most brilliant orders of chivalry, the Order of the

Charles the Bold lies in peace at the Church of Our Lady, Bruges. The glittering statue embodies the last Burgundian ruler of Flanders.

Golden Fleece. The emblem, worn around the neck, was a fleece of solid gold in recognition of the wealth generated by the cloth industry of Flanders. But the end of Burgundian rule was not far away. The last duke of Burgundy, **Charles the Bold**, was killed in battle in 1477. His daughter, Marie of Burgundy, married the Habsburg ruler of Austria, Maximilian, and the Low Countries passed to Habsburg rule.

## Flanders of the Habsburgs

From the end of Burgundian rule until the creation of the Belgian monarchy, the history of the Low Countries is confused in the extreme, as first one part, then another fell under different control through conquest or through the dynastic network which was throttling all Europe. A key element in the dynastic pattern was **Charles of Habsburg**, born in Ghent in 1500. He inherited Austria and Flanders through his grandparents Mary of Burgundy and Maximilian of Austria, while through his Spanish grandparents he inherited Spain and parts of Italy. He said wryly of himself, 'I speak German to my horse, French to my ministers and Spanish to my God.' In 1519 he became the Emperor **Charles V** by bribery. The Holy Roman Empire was to continue in name until Napoleon extinguished it in 1806, but Charles was the last effective emperor, directly controlling immense regions of Europe, from Germany to Sicily.

Flanders benefited little from its distinguished son. He spent much of his time in Spain, and in 1540 launched a ferocious attack on his native city, Ghent, over a question of taxes. Under Charles, the cloth towns of Flanders declined economically, as Bruges and Ghent not only had to combat the indifference of their rulers (who favoured Antwerp) but also saw their economy flounder in the face of competition from English cloth manufacturers. He abdicated in 1555 in favour of his son, **Philip II**, and the Low Countries were caught up in the endless wars of succession. The blackest period in Flanders' history was undoubtedly that of Spanish rule.

Philip II inherited Charles' Italian, Spanish and Netherlands possessions. Philip was a religious fanatic and bigot, who saw as his prime purpose in life the eradication of 'heresy' – i.e. the Protestantism that was rising in the north. The Inquisition was established, backed up by a ferocious soldiery to reinforce the authority of the Catholic church. In 1567 the 'Spanish Fury' occurred in Antwerp, when the unpaid, largely mercenary force ran amok in the city, looting and murdering. In response, Philip sent his army into the Netherlands, though under the terms of the **Pacification of Ghent** treaty, which guaranteed freedom of religious beliefs, Philip had to concede 17 provinces.

Antagonism continued between the Protestant north and Catholic south, until in 1579 the modern Netherlands came into being, with the declaration of independence for the predominantly Protestant United Provinces in the north, with Belgium to the south allying with the Spanish. Philip's death in 1598 brought little respite, for Flanders was caught up in the series of dynastic wars which swept through Europe: France's expansionist wars, the War of the Grand

Alliance, the War of the Spanish Succession, the War of the Austrian Succession and, finally, the Napoleonic Wars.

## Independence for Belgium

In 1815 the **Congress of Vienna**, seeking to restore order after the turmoil of the Napoleonic Wars, as one of its provisions created the United Kingdom of the Netherlands by tacking on the largely Catholic south to the Protestant United Provinces in the north. In 1830 the southern area revolted against Dutch rule, declared itself an independent state and invited Prince Leopold of Saxe-Coburg, an uncle of Queen Victoria of England, to be its first king. He reigned as **Leopold I** until 1865, establishing the present monarchy.

Flanders gained little from being part of an independent kingdom. Wealth was generated in the south, where the coal mines and heavy industries were concentrated. French influence was overwhelming. A recently published official Flemish history of modern Flanders noted: 'It is gloomy to reflect that Flemings were condemned to death in 1860 in a language they did not understand, for a crime which they did not commit, or that thousands of Flemish soldiers died in the trenches in the 1914-18 war commanded by French-speaking officers whom they could not understand.' Even as late as 1930, French was the language of the University of Ghent in the very heart of Flanders.

Flanders, together with northern France, suffered more than any other region of Europe in the First World War, for the awful trench warfare was conducted largely in the flat landscape. Remarkably, Bruges escaped almost unscathed, while its sister city of Ieper (Ypres), barely 50km (31 miles) away, was wiped out. In the Second World War the German advance was so rapid that there was relatively little damage, although Antwerp suffered rocket bombardment in the closing months of the war.

In the see-saw between north and south, post-war Flanders has emerged in the ascendancy. The heavy industry that created the wealth of Wallonia has, for the most part, closed down while, in contrast, the light industry of Flanders is flourishing, and in the ports of Ghent and Antwerp the region has vital outlets to the outside world.

## PEOPLE AND CULTURE

It is little wonder that a nation that has such a clear-cut historical divide running through its centre should defy the somewhat clichéd national characteristics which we so happily attribute to other nationalities. The Belgians are, above all, individual, and have become very adept at dealing with the language, community and political divisions within their country. They have a strong sense of history, and their pride in their cities and the role they have played is evident in the enthusiasm which they display in the many festivals and parades held throughout the region.

In towns and cities,

*Relax and take in the magnificent architecture and a beer or two in a street café, Bruges.*

religious holidays are celebrated with colourful processions and historical pageants, a tradition which in the Middle Ages would teach the illiterate Biblical stories. *Kermesse,* local fêtes held in honour of the village's patron saint, combine their religious origins with more secular attractions such as stalls, competitions and pageants.

The Flemings tend to be formal and visitors find them somewhat reserved, often mistaking this attitude for brusqueness. They will treat you courteously, but without fawning, for they regard tourism as an important part of their lives. Considering the small size of some of the cities, such as Bruges, this is just as well, for its narrow streets can become seriously overcrowded in the summer months. Yet its inhabitants go patiently about their business.

If you really want to get to know the people, take a long, leisurely meal at a café or bar which locals frequent. For it is at the table that the Flemings are at their most relaxed. Eating and drinking are fundamental to their enjoyment of life, not simply for the food itself but for the discourse that accompanies it, and makes a snack stretch into a meal lasting several hours.

## ART AND ARCHITECTURE

### Architecture

The historic architecture of Flanders reflects the sturdy independence of the burghers who made its fortune. Unlike most other European countries, it is not the palaces and castles of nobles that dominate but the civic buildings and private houses of a prosperous middle class. Apart from the churches, the great buildings function either for the running of the city – the city halls – or for the humdrum purpose of trade: cloth halls, butchers' halls, fishmarkets and the halls of the guilds that organised them. Timber and stone have always been at a premium in the flat, rather marshy terrain, but the cheapest building material of all lies underfoot – clay for the making of bricks.

It is difficult to carve brick – if decoration is required then resort is made to paint, but more usually the brick is left untouched to mellow over the centuries. It confers, too, a

*The 123m (404ft) spire of the Cathedral of Our Lady imposingly presides over the more modern, yet still traditional architecture of Antwerp.*

homogeneity on the city as a whole. In Bruges, the new brick-built Holiday Inn hotel blends in happily with its neighbours, even though it is in the Burg, the ancient heart of the city. Brick, too, can be built to a great height. The dominant feature of almost every town, great and small, is the brick-built belfort or belfry, often towering up to nearly a hundred metres.

There are few **prehistoric** remains in Flanders, for there was little here to attract small, unorganised groups. Warfare provided the stimulus, with the break-up of the Carolingian empire in the 9C. Bruges entered history in the form of a castle built to defend the hinterland from Viking raiders. The **Romanesque** period (1100-1250), characterised by massive structures with rather dark interiors, is concentrated mainly in the south, but Ghent has an excellent example in the Koornstapelhuis on the Graslei, or take a look at Bruges' Basilica of the Holy Blood. **Gothic** (13C-16C), with its soaring pinnacles and elegant arches, spread throughout the region in both churches and civic buildings. The magnificent brick and granite St Bavo's Cathedral in Ghent is a splendid example, built as a demonstration of the town's wealth resulting from the cloth trade, while the Stadhuis, Bruges, one of the oldest town halls in Belgium, has a wonderful Gothic façade, with delicately traced windows and soaring pilasters. The **Renaissance** and **Baroque** (mid-16C to end 17C) are also well represented, particularly in the field of civic architecture. Antwerp's Stadhuis by Cornelius Floris de Vriendt combines Flemish features with Italian Renaissance. Alongside all these grand civic buildings and glorious churches is a wonderfully harmonious blend of houses, with their stepped gables in different heights contrasting yet blending together with those with Gothic-style façades and pinnacles. Most are built of brick, and in Bruges you will notice that the shutters are characteristically dark red.

## The Begijnhof (Beguinages)

There is no English translation for this word, for there has never been anything similar among English-speaking nations. They came into being during the Crusades, probably about the year 1180 when a priest of Liege, Lambert le Begue, founded an almshouse or hospital to care for the widows and orphaned daughters of Crusaders. Their administration resembled that of nunneries but the Beguines, as the residents were called, did not take vows and were free to leave at any time. Beguinages were widespread throughout the Continent but after the Reformation fell out of favour. The best surviving examples today are in Flanders, and their peaceful atmosphere and quiet green areas create a unique and almost other-worldly respite from the hustle and bustle of the surrounding streets.

## Art

In 1994, the city of Bruges was host to the world in order to commemorate the 500th anniversary of the death of Hans Memling. For a week, art historians and journalists from Japan to Britain, from the US to Russia, flocked into the city to admire Memling's work which had been brought back to Bruges from all over the world. For over 500 years, from the realism of Jan van

Eyck (15C), Bouts, Van der Weyden and Metsys (16C), Jordaens and Teniers (17C) to Ensor (20C), Flanders has been a well-spring and guardian of art.

The political confusion of the past makes it difficult to 'place' a Flemish artist. Some were born in what is today France, Holland or even Germany but, whatever their origins, their work developed into a recognisable school. From the beginning, the enormous popularity of that work has meant that foreign patrons vied with each other to obtain examples, so that 'Flemish art' is to be found in all the world's major galleries. But so prolific were the artists, and so aware of their heritage were the cities, that the galleries and churches of Bruges, Antwerp and Ghent are treasure houses of the work of Old Masters.

Flemish art, as we know it, developed with astonishing rapidity. Before the 15C there was little in the way of 'easel' pictures. Artists found their chief expression through stained-glass windows and illumination in manuscripts, and Gothic art of the period was primarily religious, but with realistic backgrounds and a very earthy intention to flatter powerful people. A popular religious art form was the diptych, triptych or polytych, an altarpiece consisting of two or more painted panels, frequently named after the donor, and set above and behind the altar. Over the centuries the panels tended to be separated and sold individually. The organisers of the Memling Exhibition, for instance, had to approach museums in Italy and the US, as well as the Groeninge Museum in Bruges itself in order to assemble the three panels of the Triptych of Jan Crabbe.

# Four Great Flemish Artists

***Jan van Eyck*** *(c1390-1441)*
Although it is improbable that van Eyck personally invented the technique of oil painting, his genius brought it to such a high level that the great painters of Italy eagerly adopted it and its use spread throughout Europe. Born near Maastricht in Holland, in his early 30s he became painter to the cultured and powerful Philip the Good, Duke of Burgundy at the Burgundian court in Lille. He was also the Duke's *valet de chambre*, a trusted confidante, and as such undertook diplomatic missions which gave him a wide contact with European art and architecture. He settled in Bruges in 1430, but retained contact with the court until his death. His paintings are easy to identify, for he had the engaging habit of including some such remark as 'Jan van Eyck made me' or 'Jan van Eyck was here.'

***Hans Memling*** *(c1430-94)*
Memling was German by birth, but settled in Bruges some time in his mid-20s. He was registered as a citizen in 1465 and was so successful that he became one of the city's largest taxpayers. The wealthy foreign merchants who made their headquarters in Bruges were among his patrons. So popular was his work that today it is scattered throughout the world, but many of his most important works remain in Flanders, in particular Bruges (in the Sint-Janshospitaal, or the Memling Museum). His work has a strong religious theme, characterised by gentleness. He also excelled in portraiture. Curiously, apart from the religious paintings, only one portrait of a female survives, that of a young woman in Sint-Janshospitaal.

***Pieter Brueghel*** *(c1525-69)*
Although he had the highest social connections, the artist was sometimes called 'Peasant' Brueghel because of his obsession with rural life. He was a Master of the Antwerp Guild in 1551 and later travelled widely through France and Italy, although he was never influenced by the Renaissance. His work is in dramatic contrast with the courtly world of van Eyck and

Memling, depicting as it does the daily life and interests of ordinary people. Several works are displayed in Antwerp's Fine Arts Museum, and his famous portrayal of *Dulle Griet* (Mad Meg) can be seen in Museum Mayer van den Berg.

*Hellish detail from* Dulle Griet *(Mad Meg) by Pieter Brueghel (Museum Mayer van den Berg).*

### Pieter Paul Rubens *(1577-1640)*

A highly successful business-man and diplomat as well as artist, Rubens was born of an Antwerp family in exile in Cologne, Germany. All his adult life he moved in aristo-cratic circles, in particular in the ducal courts of Italy where he absorbed the art of the High Renaissance, becoming the foremost Baroque artist of his time. His first major com-mission was the decoration of the Jesuit church of St Carolus Borromeus in Antwerp. The Cathedral of Our Lady, Antwerp, has the lavishly Baroque *Raising of the Cross*, *Descent from the Cross* and the *Resurrection*. His prolific output of work was made possible only by employing a team of highly talented assistants whose work he kept under close control. His second wife, Helena Fourment, whom he married when she was 16, features in many of his mythologies and portraits. He gained his knighthood from Charles I of England, to whom he was sent on a diplomatic mission.

The impetus for the new art came from the presence of a wealthy and cultured court, that of Philip the Good, Duke of Burgundy, in Lille in the early 15C, and the invention of oil painting. The invention has been ascribed to Jan van Eyck, but it is unlikely that any one artist made so great a leap. Linseed oil had occasionally been used as a binding agent since the 10C, but it was not until the early 15C that its use became widespread in Flanders. The previous medium of tempera (a mixture of powder colour, water and egg-yolk) dried very rapidly so it was extremely difficult to create detail. Oil-based painting, drying very slowly, allowed thin layers to be laid one above the other, which created both an impression of depth and dried to an almost enamel-like brilliance which would last for centuries. While he retained the religious element of the Gothic tradition of art, the new medium of oil paints enabled van Eyck to create an astonishing degree of detail. Never before had artists observed so minutely, reproduced with such accurate realism or used perspective in an innovative way. In his painting *The Madonna with Canon van der Paele* (in Bruges' Groeningemuseum, *see* p.68), the Canon is shown holding an eyeglass over a book. By looking through the eyeglass, it is just possible to read the words.

Given the detail that oil-paintings allowed, portraiture is outstanding. In van Eyck's painting of the *Arnolfini Wedding* (now in London's National Gallery) the husband appears smugly self-satisfied, the wife demurely submissive – until one realises that there is a glint in her eye and a set of her mouth which suggests her husband is by no means going to have it all his own way.

The Mystic Marriage of St Catherine, *Triptych by Hans Memling (Memlingmuseum, Bruges).*

The Flemish landscape was the setting for the accurately observed paintings of Pieter Brueghel the Elder (c1525-69). The great period of Flemish Old Masters came to an end in the 17C with the exuberant work of three Antwerp artists – Pieter Paul Rubens (1577-1640), and his successors Anthony van Dyck (1599-1641) and Jacob Jordaens (1593-1678). The 18C was generally a period of stagnation, but Belgium's proclamation of independence stimulated renewed creativity in the 19C with an emphasis on nationalism, well reflected in the work of the aristocratic painter, Henri Leys (1815-69), in his murals in Antwerp's Stadhuis.

The 20C has seen a vigorous development of Expressionism with individuals such as Ensor, the Sint Martens-Latem group, and Surrealism (Permeke). Antwerp's Museum voor Schone Kunsten (Fine Art Museum) has a large collection of modern Belgian art.

## ANTWERPEN★★★ (ANTWERP)

Despite being the second largest city in
Belgium, Antwerp is relatively easy to get to
know, for its historic centre along the bank
of the Scheldt is compact. It consists of three
linked squares clustered around the
cathedral: the large, rather characterless
Groenplaats, the charming little triangular
Handschoenmarkt (Old Glove Market), and
the handsome Grote Markt. A long, straight
boulevard consisting of linked quays
(kaaien) runs along the riverside and is
joined, to north and south, by major traffic
arteries following the lines of the now-
demolished city walls. Within this roughly
D-shaped area are most places of historic

*The Bronze
fountain in Grote
Market (1887), by
Antwerp sculptor
Jef Lambeaux,
depicts Silvius
Brabo casting the
giant Druon
Antigon's severed
hand into the
Scheldt.*

interest. With two exceptions, all the buildings and places listed below are within a comfortable half-hour's walk from the centre.

Although a pedestrian tunnel was constructed under the Scheldt in 1933, the left bank was not developed until the 1960s. The development there is mostly in the square-cut, mass-produced architectural style which swept across Europe in the post-war years. If time permits, however, it is perhaps worthwhile crossing the river in order to look back and see Antwerp's peerless skyline, a perfect medieval profile. The only thing that challenges the delicate majesty of the cathedral's incredible tower is the massive, squat mass of the Boerentoren (Farmers' Tower), built 1929-32 and claimed to be Europe's first skyscraper.

## The Birth of Antwerp

In the Grote Markt is a large fountain topped with the figure of a man hurling a severed hand. The symbol of hands also appears on the city's coat of arms. It arises from a legend which seeks to explain the origins of Antwerp's name. In Dutch, *handwerpen* means 'hand throw', and the legend goes that a giant, Druon Antigon, used to dominate this bend of the river, taking toll of all ships passing along and cutting off the hand of anyone unable to pay. A Roman soldier, Silvius Brabo, killed the giant and hurled his hand into the river. Folk memory invariably distorts but does not entirely invent. The legend reflects the fact that the paying of tolls was an important source of income and that, unlike most Flemish towns, the Romans had a part in the founding of Antwerp.

The city's name explains why it came into existence at exactly this spot. The river, sweeping round in a great curve, left alluvial deposits on the right bank which formed a firm, flat headland, the *aanwerp*. Although Gallo-Romano remains dating from the 2C-3C have been found on the river bank near the Steen, the main development was in the 9C when Antwerp was part of Lotharingia, subject to the emperor. Beyond the river the Counts of Flanders, vassals of the King of France, held sway.

In the Middle Ages Antwerp's greatest rivals were Bruges and Ghent, but gradually the city drew ahead, partly through its incomparable position as a port, and partly because its guilds did not pursue such a constrictive policy as those of its rivals. Culturally, the city's Golden Age in the 16C coincided with its political and economic nadir. The clash between Catholics and Protestants, and the attempts of the Spanish to regain control of the Netherlands, contributed to its decline. The Spanish re-captured the city in 1585, and nearly half the inhabitants (the Protestants) fled northward, the population falling from 100 000 to 42 000. The Dutch closed the Scheldt, strangling the city's

*The original 16C printing machinery of Europe's foremost print works can be seen in Museum Plantin-Moretus.*

trade. Yet ironically this was also the period when the painters like Rubens, Jordaens and van Dyck all flourished; the printer Christopher Plantin set up his workshop; and the Catholic Counter-Reformation displayed itself in the flamboyant, self-confident Baroque of innumerable churches.

## Napoleonic Period

The occupation of the city by French revolutionaries from 1792 brought some economic revival but also cultural disaster. Napoleon's intention to turn the city into a launching pad against England led to the revival of the port and an attempt to open the Scheldt, but the anti-clerical fervour of the revolutionaries resulted in the plundering of those churches whose pastors refused to sign an oath of allegiance to the republic. Culture was Gallicised, with street names translated into French and the printing of Dutch texts forbidden.

The Scheldt was closed again in 1830 during the Belgian Revolution, but in 1833 it re-opened. Ten years later a rail link to Cologne, the *IJzeren Rijn* (Iron Rhine) was built, and Antwerp began a period of explosive growth, swelling from 90 000 inhabitants in 1850 to 300 000 in 1906. Wealthy merchants were tempted back, creating beautiful residential areas in the suburbs to the south and east. Antwerp appeared on the European stage once again as a major city.

**The Sinjoren** is the nickname given to the citizens of Antwerp and dates from the Golden Age of the 16C when, according to the Spanish, the wealthy merchants lived like lords (*señores*, corrupted into 'sinjeurs').

## EXPLORING THE CITY

Antwerp's cultural treasure is overwhelming. There are no fewer than 43 museums, including such specialist museums as one for Rhetoric and another for Anaesthesia. There are ten major churches, each with outstanding artistic works, and 26 important historical buildings – quite apart from the countless number with something unusual about them. Those attractions described here are necessarily only a selection which really should be seen if time permits. The Must See list is a further selection of those which *must* be seen on the briefest of visits. There is an entrance fee for most of the museums (a combination ticket allows three to be visited for the price of two, and can be purchased at any of the ten participating urban museums), and most are closed on Mondays.

*Return of the prodigal son – Antwerp's own Baroque artist, Pieter Paul Rubens, commemorated in Groenplaats.*

### Must See

**Onze Lieve Vrouw Kathedraal★★★** (Cathedral of Our Lady)
**Museum Mayer van den Berg★★**, museum of Medieval and Renaissance art
**Museum Plantin-Moretus★★★**, a 16C printing house and mansion
**Hendrik Conscienceplein★**, an exquisite little square, with the Baroque church of **St Carolus Borromeus★**
**Koninklijk Museum voor Schone Kunsten★★★** (Royal Museum of Fine Arts)
**Rubenshuis★★**, home of Antwerp's famous citizen

### AROUND THE CATHEDRAL

Begin your exploration of this historic area in **Groenplaats** which, as its name implies, was once an open green space, originally a large churchyard. Locals delight in re-telling macabre stories of the discoveries made in the 1960s, when it was excavated to make the present immense underground car park and tram station. This is a major stop on the tramways, with the main railway station just ten minutes away.

*The illuminated Cathedral of Our Lady dominates the night cityscape.*

The statue in the centre is of the city's most famous citizen, Pieter Paul Rubens. The immense Hilton Hotel, originally a department store, dominates the south side. The cafés on the north side of the square provide animation to an otherwise dull picture.

The first-time visitor to Antwerp in search of a meal would do well to make for the little square of **Handschoenmarkt**. Here, and in the adjoining lanes, cafés, bars and restaurants stand side by side, offering a tremendous choice. Although it is manifestly a tourist area, prices are not much higher than elsewhere. The beautiful well-head in the square is the work of the artist Quentin Metsys (1464-1530), who began his career as a metal-worker. Opposite the square is Oude Koormarkt. Look out for the portal at No 16 through which is the delightful **Vlaaikensgang★**, a picturesque street with a village atmosphere.

**Map of Antwerp**

**A**  Sint-Elisabethgasthuiskapel
**B**  Sint-Niklaaskapel
**D**  Vleeshuis
**E**  Oude Beurs
**H**  Stadhuis
**M¹**  Etnografisch Museum
**M²**  Volkskundemuseum
**M³**  Maagdenhuis
**M⁴**  Rockoxhuis
**T¹**  De Poesje

Terrace cafés front the Cathedral of Our Lady, home to some of Rubens' superior works.

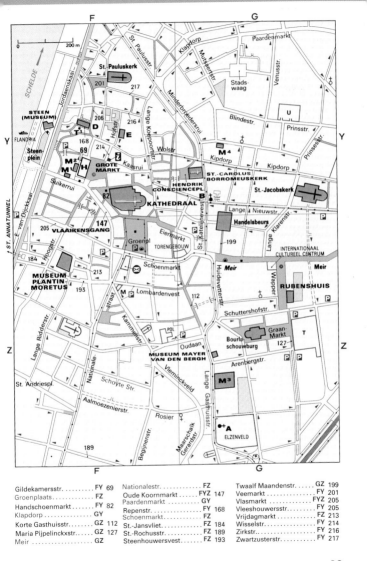

It is difficult to appreciate the size of the **Onze Lieve Vrouw Kathedraal★★★** (Cathedral of Our Lady), hemmed in as it is by houses, but it is the largest and, perhaps, the most beautiful church in Belgium. It has only recently completed a quarter of a century of restoration. On the right-hand side of the façade is a life-size modern bronze group, showing one of its architects, Jan Appelmans, and masons at work in the mid-15C. The group vividly conveys the fact that this vast building, together with its delicate, lace-like tower, was created by men using the most elementary of tools, making its achievement even more awe-inspiring.

Inside, in the north transept, is an excellent series of models showing the development of the building in stages over some two centuries. The first stage was the construction of the choir in the early 15C; the last was the completion of the **tower★★★** around 1521. This rises to a height of 123m (404ft) and contains a carillon of 47 bells, together with eight great bells, one named 'the Carolus' after the Emperor Charles V.

The **interior** has a cool, serene beauty, accentuated by the use of white and the sheer scale of the building – it is 117m (380ft) long by 65m (211ft) wide. A severe fire in 1533, the destructiveness of the Iconoclasts in 1566 and, finally, the plundering by the French who auctioned off whatever was removable, means that there are few pre-18C survivals. The cathedral authorities have been painstakingly re-assembling what can be tracked down. As recently as 1995, five marble reliefs from behind the High Altar turned up in the auction house of Christies, London, and have now been reinstated.

*Painstakingly restored, the magnificent nave and high-arched ceilings of the Cathedral of our Lady accent the grandeur of this architectural achievement.*

Yet considerable artistic treasures remain; a printed list identifying these is available at the entrance. The most famous are undoubtedly the four great paintings by Rubens, in particular *The Raising of the Cross* (1610) on the north transept and, on the south side, *The Descent from the Cross* (1612), painted immediately after his return from Italy and showing the influence of the Italian masters. (Note that there is an entry charge to the cathedral, whose main entrance is in the Handschoenmarkt. Open Mon-Fri, 10am-5pm; Sat, 10am-3pm; Sun, 1-4pm.)

*Visitors admire the Biblical grandiosity of Rubens' The Raising of the Cross, in the Cathedral of Our Lady.*

Just a few steps away and dominated by the soaring tower of the Cathedral is **Grote Markt★**. Only Brussels' Grand-Place can equal this among Flemish cities. It is the municipal heart of Antwerp with the magnificent Renaissance **Stadhuis** (City Hall) – still the centre of government – and the towering façades of the 16C **guild houses,** each with its gilded symbol, ranged side by side. Many of these latter buildings are restorations (or even reconstructions based on documentary evidence) but done so well that it takes an expert to spot the difference. Among the originals are: no 3,

*Flags decorate the façade of Antwerp's distinguished City Hall, in Grote Markt.*

Den Engel (the Angel), with a lively tavern on its ground floor; nos 7 and 9, the Oude en Jonge Handboog (Old and New Crossbowmen), with the figures of St George and the Dragon; and no 38, De Gulden Balans (The Golden Scales).

Dominating the west side is the City Hall, built 1561-64. Although it was designed by a Fleming, Cornelis Floris de Vriendt, he had Italian associates and the Stadhuis introduced a Flemish Renaissance style that was widely copied. Gutted by fire during the Spanish Fury of 1576, it was rebuilt by 1579 and has since been restored on successive occasions, the last major restoration being 1880-84. (Public access to the historic areas is by guided tours only.)

*Italian influence pervades the opulent interior of City Hall.*

## WEST OF GROTE MARKT

Although Antwerp draws its wealth primarily from the Scheldt, the city turns its back upon the river, probably because of the cold north-east wind. There is, however, much to see on the quays lining the river bank. The quays are the work of Napoleon; they replace the irregular waterfront that was the original port and were completed in the 1880s. Historically, the port has moved steadily northward, as attested by the rows of open warehouses with their beautiful ironwork, now standing forlorn and empty and frequently used as car parks.

A fortification first appeared on the banks of the Scheldt in the 9C as part of the defences between Lotharingia and West Francia. These remains date from c1200, making **Het Steen** (The Castle) the oldest surviving building in the city. It was part of a much larger castle, built to defend the walled town centre and the *aanwerp*. Restored by Charles V in 1520, it was used as a prison until 1823. Much of it was

*The impressive Het Steen (Castle) presides over the Scheldt, guarded by an image of the legendary stretchable man, Lange Wapper.*

demolished during the building of the quays. Today it houses the **Nationaal Scheepvaartmuseum★** (National Maritime Museum), a beguiling collection of exhibits relating to maritime life and Antwerp's special relationship with the sea. Part of the museum is on the adjacent wharves, where real ships can be visited. (Open Tue-Sun, 10am-4.45pm.)

The quirky statue in front of the Museum is of Lange Wapper, a rather dubious legendary figure who had the power to extend himself and so peer into bedroom windows. Nearby is the *Flandria* quay, where river tours begin (*see* p.96).

A few hundred metres south, on St-Jansvliet, is the entrance to the pedestrian tunnel which passes under the Scheldt, the **St Annatunnel**, with two flights of escalators. It still has its 1933 woodwork, together with original artwork. Motorcycles can be taken down but not ridden through the tunnel. Its 500m (547yd) length is monitored by TV.

*Life on the ocean wave – investigate Antwerp's maritime past at the National Maritime Museum.*

## NORTH OF GROTE MARKT

Approached from Jordaenskaai by the short Vleeshuisstraat is the **Vleeshuis★** (Butchers' Hall). The headquarters of the powerful Butchers' Guild, it is an outstanding brick building constructed 1501-04. The magnificent hall on the ground floor is constructed entirely in brick, with a vaulted roof supported by pillars. It was the only place where meat could be sold; the guild officers met on the upper floor. Today it houses a **museum** of folk art, archaeology and local history. The ground floor has an outstanding collection of wood carvings in the Germanic tradition, ranging from the 16C-18C, among them a super satyr, contrasting with the many figures of saints. Access to the upper floor is by a very narrow spiral staircase. On display is jewellery, furniture and the **musical instruments★** in which Antwerp specialised. (Open Tue-Sun, 10am-4.45pm.)

*Now the swine have gone it's easier to admire the museum of folk culture and the amazing brick architecture at Butchers' Hall.*

*The three-tiered façade of St Carolus Borromeus adjoins the delightful cobbled square of Hendrik Conscienceplein.*

A few minutes' walk to the north through narrow, rather run-down streets, is the **Veemarkt** (Cattle Market) and **St Pauluskerk★** (St Paul's Church). Built in the Baroque 16C style, the church has suffered both fire and vandalism but the interior houses important woodcarvings and paintings, among them works by Rubens, van Dyck and Jordaens.

The exquisite little cobbled square of **Hendrik Conscienceplein★**, with the superb church of **St Carolus Borromeus★**, is a showpiece of the historic area. The exuberant Baroque façade of the church, in the style pioneered by the Jesuits, is reputed to be the work of Rubens. The church was built 1615-21, its interior richly decorated by Rubens. A fire in 1718 destroyed much of the interior, including Rubens' ceiling paintings, although the apse survived, together with the Lady Chapel and the coloured marble which was a major feature of the church. Opposite is the **Municipal Library**, once part of the monastic complex. The Librarian was the 19C novelist Hendrik Conscience, whose statue is in the square.

Across the way, on Keizerstraat 12, is the

**Rockoxhuis★** (Rockox House). The home of a 17C mayor of Antwerp, Nikolaas Rockox, art collector and friend of Rubens, it was acquired by a trust in 1949. Using a detailed inventory, the trust was able to furnish and decorate the house in an authentic 17C manner, to include a unique collection of furniture, ceramics and paintings which include works by Rubens, van Dyck, Jordaens, Teniers, Bruegel the Younger and Metsys. (Open Tue-Sun, 10am-5pm.)

Continuing east, away from the Scheldt, is the final resting place of many of Antwerp's rich and famous, **St Jacobskerk** (St James' Church), on Lange Nieustraat. The building of this church went on for 165 years, from 1491 to 1656. It escaped the usual plunder by French revolutionaries, for although the pastor refused to sign the oath of allegiance, a chaplain was found to do so. The **interior★**,

*Latin-inscribed flagstones lead up to Rubens' Chapel in St James' Church. Having painted the altarpiece in readiness, Rubens was installed in a vault here after his death.*

with its 23 chapels, is consequently bursting with works of art (a descriptive list is available). The **Rubens Chapel** behind the main altar is of particular interest. It was commissioned by Rubens' second wife, Helena Fourment, two years after his death in 1640. In 1645 his coffin was placed in a vault which would in time be occupied by 42 members of his family. Rubens painted the altarpiece himself as a funerary monument, and the figures are believed to represent members of his family with Rubens himself as St George, his little son Frans the Baby Jesus, Isabella Brandt, his first wife as the Madonna and Helena Fourment as Mary Magdalene.

## SOUTH OF GROTE MARKT

### Museum Plantin-Moretus★★★
*Vrijdagmarkt 22*
Arguably this is the most important museum of printing in Europe, for it illustrates the moment when printing emerged as a major commercial as well as cultural force.

*Lush ornamental gardens fill the central courtyard of the Museum Plantin-Moretus, once the premier printing establishment in Europe.*

*Frozen in time for four centuries, as if the master has just stepped out for a few minutes, the office and presses of the legendary printer Christopher Plantin.*

Christopher Plantin came to Antwerp from France in 1548 and set up his printing house in this mansion in 1576. In it, 1 860 works 'in all the languages of Christendom', were published. It is also a family home, which adds greatly to its interest. Be sure to pick up the printed leaflet available in reception. The museum is brilliantly laid out, with all exhibits relating to each other, but without the explanatory leaflet it can be confusing.

The rectangular mansion is built round a formal garden. In the room used by proof-readers are displays of printed sheets with the original hand-written corrections. The south and east wings are the family quarters, and the original bookshop, complete with counter and list of books prohibited by the Vatican, is in the east wing. The great saloon contains family portraits of the Plantins by Rubens. In the adjoining room are priceless illuminated manuscripts showing the development of print from handwriting. (Open Tue-Sun, 10am-4.45pm.)

### Museum Mayer van den Berg★★
*Lange Gasthuisstraat 19*
Fritz Mayer van den Bergh died at the age of 43 in 1901, and his mother built this jewel-box of a museum in the 16C style to house his priceless collection of medieval and Renaissance art. Even if the building were empty it would be worth a visit for its fireplaces of multi-coloured marbles, its embossed wall hangings and its richly carved woodwork. Allow as much time as possible for, although a private collection, it can equal anything in a national museum. Particularly important is its collection of Flemish Primitives, including the famous **Dulle Griet★★** (Mad Meg), by Pieter

Brueghel, showing the terrifying mad woman against a hellish background (*see* p.23). Other artists include Quentin Metsys, Joos van Cleeve and work from the school of Rubens. (Open Tue-Sun, 10am-4.45pm; closed for restoration until March 1999.)

*The heavily ornate interior of Museum Mayer van den Berg is a fitting setting for its exquisite private collection of fine arts.*

### Maagdenhuis (Maidens' House)
*Lange Gasthuisstraat 33*
This museum contains poignant relics from the time when it was used as an orphanage

for girls (16C-17C). Look for the model which shows how an abandoned baby would be placed in a kind of drawer in the street wall and pushed inside. The mother frequently left identification in the form of half a playing card, or similar token, hoping to match it later and reclaim the child. A glass case contains many of these cards – some matched up. Also on display are what have now become valuable art objects, the gifts of benefactors. (Open daily, except Tue, 1-5pm.) The same ticket allows access to the 15C **Sint-Elisabethgasthuiskapel** (St Elisabeth Chapel) and 17C interior of the nearby **Elzenveld** (St Elisabeth Hospital), now a conference and cultural centre which organises exhibitions. Adjoining it is the **Botanical Garden**, developed in 1804 from the original medieval herb garden.

**Rubenshuis** ★★ (Rubens' House) *Wapper*
The pleasant walk between Maagdenhuis and Rubenshuis is punctuated by peaceful squares, restaurants and theatres. The house itself reflects Rubens' status as perhaps the richest and most successful painter of his day. He bought the house in 1610, later adding a large studio where he both worked and taught, and an art gallery where he displayed paintings and sculptures. The present house is a noteworthy piece of restoration, for it was virtually a derelict shell when the city acquired it in 1937, and provides an interesting insight into a wealthy 17C household. There are only ten of the 600 works from Rubens' own hand on display but they include his self-portrait and some personal belongings. There are also works by his contemporaries. (Open Tue-Sun, 10am-4.45pm.)

## ZUID QUARTER (SOUTH)

*The next two museums are relatively distant. Take tram no 8, or bus 23 or 29 from Groenplaats.*

The **Koninklijk Museum voor Schone Kunsten★★★** (Royal Museum of Fine Arts) is in Leopold de Waelplaats. This massive neo-Classical building was constructed as a central feature of the Zuid quarter, laid out 1884-90. Although located just outside the city centre, this museum should not be missed. The origin of the collection was the works of art looted by the French revolutionaries at the end of the 18C and later restored. Subsequent additions have made it a major representative collection of Flemish art, from the 14C to the present day. Highlights include works by Memling and Brueghel, *Madonna at the Fountain* by van Eyck and *Flight into Egypt* by Patinir, with contemporary works by Magritte and Delvaux. An audio gallery guide in English, Dutch and French is available as part of the entrance fee, and provides information about the most important works.

*In a spacious, relaxed setting, admire the Flemish works housed in the Royal Museum of Fine Arts.*

A few minutes' walk away is the **Museum van Hedendaagse Kunst Antwerpen**

**(MUHKA)** (Museum of Contemporary Art Antwerp), housed in a converted grain silo on Leuvenstraat and containing modern works from 1970 onwards.

## EAST OF CENTRE

The broad, handsome **Meir** and its extension De Keyserlei, the city's modern 'high street' with its exuberant turn-of-the-century architecture, leads to the **Central Railway Station**. Built between 1900-1905 by direct command of the king, Leopold II, this cathedral-like building is one of the last great survivors of Europe's railway age.

Just behind the station, on Koningin Astridplein, is one of the world's oldest and best known zoos. **Antwerp Zoo★★** has more than 4 000 animals, and its open spaces and green areas offer a respite from the city

*Catching a train is almost a religious experience at the monumental Central Railway Station, with its 60m (197ft) high dome.*

bustle. The zoo is internationally renowned for its scientific research and breeding programmes for threatened species, and its art deco buildings include a planatarium, nocturama, aquarium, botanical greenhouse and several restaurants. (Open daily, 9am-3/6.15pm; combined tickets are available with a river trip on *Flandria, see* p.96.)

## Diamond Quarter

At first sight there is little in this area of rather shabby buildings to indicate that this is the world's largest diamond market. Then you notice that the small shop windows are blazing with gems, and that some of the streets are not open to the public. Jews, in their distinctive Hassidic garments, sweep past, a messenger hurries by with an attaché case discreetly attached by a chain. The **Provinciaal Diamantmuseum** (Provincial Diamond Museum) tells the story (*see* p.52).

## Zurenborg★

Tram no 11 from the Central Station will take you to this residential area, which was in the open country when it was founded in the late 19C. At the centre is the fantastic Cogels-Osylei, around which are six streets of houses in the Belle Epoque style, built at the turn of the century and resembling a film set. Rich bourgeoisie indulged their fancies by building immense mansions in styles ranging from Ancient Greek to art nouveau. The area was scheduled for demolition in the 1960s but vigorous action on the part of residents ensured that it is now a protected heritage.

   South of Zurenborg, just outside the Ring, the **Openluchtmuseum voor Beeldhouwkunst Middelheim★** (Open-Air

Sculpture Museum of Middleheim) is worth a visit. The permanent collection of over 300 sculptures is set in scenic parkland, and includes works by Rodin, Rik Wouters and Raymond Duchamp-Villon.

## HAVEN (HARBOUR)

An aerial view of Antwerp shows the modern city, large though it is, as a kind of appendage to the immense port stretching north almost to the Dutch border. In the 1890s there were about 16km (10 miles) of quays: today there are 127km (79 miles). It is now Europe's second-largest port, handling over 110 million tonnes of cargo and servicing over 1 500 vessels annually. It has the world's biggest dock and second-largest petrochemical industry. All this is the creation of the great river. When you stand on an embankment of the Scheldt just north of the city and look north across the bend of the river, it is difficult to realise that the open sea is more than 70km (44 miles) away.

*Fanciful architecture in the Zurenborg.*

To appreciate the port fully, a guided boat tour is recommended (*see* p.96). However, the interesting area immediately north of the historic centre is easily accessible on foot.

The two oldest surviving docks, today known as **Bonapartedok** and **Willemdok**, were dug by Napoleon as part of his plan to create that 'pistol aimed at the heart of England', as he described Antwerp. Then came the much larger **Kattendijkdok**, built 1860-81 at right angles to the Napoleonic docks. The area between and around these docks became known as **'t Eilandje** (the Little Island) and has become almost a living museum of industrial archaeology, with its maritime equipment and warehouses mostly dating from the 19C.

## Diamonds

Diamonds began to be cut in Bruges in the 14C from stones imported from India, via Venice. The trade shifted to Antwerp in the 16C after Bruges' harbour silted up. Jewish diamond merchants fleeing persecution in Portugal and Spain found refuge in Antwerp and, in the 19C, were reinforced by refugees from Eastern Europe, further developing the industry. Antwerp's diamond quarter is known as the 'Jerusalem of the North', because it has the largest settlement of orthodox Jews in this part of Europe. Today, the city handles more than 70 per cent of the world's total diamond trade, with 1 500 different concerns employing some 30 000 people. The heart of the trade in Antwerp is the Diamond Quarter – a small area whose financial turnover is quite considerable.

*Diamonds are a girl's best friend.*

**museum** (Provincial Diamond Museum), run by the Province of Antwerp, in Lange Herentalsestraat 31-33, demonstrates the processes of the industry, from mining to the finished product, and includes a reconstruction of a 19C diamond workshop. There is a 'treasure room' showing priceless antique and modern jewellery. On Saturday afternoons (1.30-4.30pm), a diamond cutter and polisher gives demonstrations (museum open daily, 10am-5pm).

The rough stones, mostly coming from Africa, are either cleft or sawn to gain the most valuable shape. They are then polished to give the 57 facets which create the characteristic brilliance unique to diamonds. All aspects of the trade are firmly under the control of the *Hoge Raad voor Diamant* (Diamond High Council), which issues the vital certificate of authenticity for each stone.

The **Provinciaal Diamant-**

*Left: Examining diamonds.*
*Right: Rough diamond polishing.*

## BRUGGE★★★ (BRUGES)

Bruges is relatively young among European cities. It enters history about the end of the 9C when Baldwin of the Iron Arm, Count of Flanders, built a fortress as protection against the Norsemen. A city began to develop around the fort and, despite its late

*The 15C Gothic-style City Hall is decorated with statues of the counts and countesses of Flanders.*

start, Bruges grew with astonishing speed. Between the 13C and 15C it became the most important centre of trade in northern Europe. In 1340 it had 35 000 inhabitants; only Paris and a few Italian cities had larger populations at that time. The staple trade was the wool for the Flemish cloth industries, which Bruges was in an ideal position to import from the major centres of production in England. Merchants from 20 different nations settled in the city, their wealth spilling over to adorn it with beautiful buildings. The various nationalities formed groups. In 1322, for instance, the Venetians established an organisation which would develop into the world's first Stock Exchange or Bourse. In 1475 William Caxton, a member of the English 'nation' in the city, published the first book in the English language.

The Golden Age of Bruges was during the period of the Dukes of Burgundy in the 15C. Some of the city's greatest buildings – including the Stadhuis (City Hall) and Onze Lieve Vrouwekerk (Church of Our Lady) – were built, rebuilt or completed during this exuberant period. The last great Burgundian festival took place in Bruges in 1468, when Duke Charles the Bold married Margaret of York, sister of Edward IV of England. At this sumptuous wedding, it was recorded, an entire orchestra was accommodated in an enormous pastry, 40 singers sat in the belly of a whale, a gigantic unicorn appeared with a leopard on its back, the fountains ran with the red and white wine of Burgundy and the streets were decorated by artists such as Hans Memling and Hugo van der Goes.

The spectacle, in fact, marked the

beginning of the end of both Burgundian rule in Flanders and Bruges' prosperity. Charles the Bold was killed at the Battle of Nancy in 1477, and his daughter Mary, reluctantly accepted by the citizens as successor, was killed in a riding accident in 1482. Towards the end of the century, the river Zwin – Bruges' lifeline to the sea – began to silt up and trade began to decline.

By the early 19C trade had died completely and Bruges was a ghost city, the splendid mansions empty, the churches deserted, the canals abandoned. The establishment of the port of Zeebrugge (Bruges-by-the-Sea) in 1895 helped to revive trade but it was tourism which brought the

city back to life. Paradoxically, it benefited from the long period of neglect. The Industrial Revolution passed Bruges by, and the booming tourist industry of the 20C rediscovered a perfectly preserved medieval and Renaissance city.

Tourism today is Bruges' major industry. It has, of course, brought its problems. In the high season hotels, restaurants, museums and streets are packed, and it is certainly advisable to avoid this period. But Bruges has not been fossilised. It still belongs to its citizens. Families on bicycles weave in and out of the endless lines of horse-drawn tourist coaches; restaurants and taverns continue to serve Flemish fare.

Bruges derives its Flemish name from the multiplicity of bridges that cross the canals that are so characteristic of the city. In the past, however, the one thing that marred the city's attraction was the smell from them. They were only a few feet deep, and the combination of muddy bottoms and an indifferent sewage system created unpleasant effluvia, particularly when the water was stirred up by motorboats. A massive reconstruction of the sewage system has meant that Bruges is now as wholesome as it is beautiful.

*Built along canals, Bruges' timeless appeal lies in its peaceful, picturesque waterways.*

## EXPLORING THE CITY

The city is almost an island, ringed by a canal. Within the island, either the streets are traffic-free or pedestrians have priority. A green belt, the Vesten, following the ramparts, now entirely circles the city, so that it is possible to take a leisurely walk all the way round, savouring the picturesque views which greet you at each turn, or you can bicycle along the parallel roads.

Despite its compact layout, there is much to see in Bruges. Below is a selection of some of the key sights you should try to see, though how much you fit in will depend on the length of your stay.

Whatever you decide to make your priorities, do take a boat trip on the canals, for it will not only give you an insight into the urban layout, but is a relaxing, romantic and enlightening way to get a feel for this picturesque city.

**Must See**
**Heilige Bloed Basiliek★** (Holy Blood Basilica) in the **Burg★★**
**Onze Lieve Vrouwekerk★** (Church of Our Lady), with tombs of Charles the Bold and his daughter Mary and sculpture by Michelangelo
**Groeningemuseum★★★** on the Dijver
**Memlingmuseum★★★** in Sint-Janshospitaal
**Begijnhof★★**
**Boat trip★★★** on the canals
**Belfort★★★** and **Hallen★★★**

*A horse-drawn carriage is a romantic and traditional way to discover Bruges.*

## CENTRAL BRUGES
### Markt** (Market)

For centuries this has been the social heart of the town. Tournaments were held here, in Bruges' main square. From the balcony of the Belfry local laws were promulgated. Beneath it, convicts were pilloried – or executed. It was, and still is, a magnificent main square, lined with the imposing façades of the halls which once housed the city guilds. It was the city's principal marketplace from 985 until 1983, when the market was transferred to 't Zand. In the high season today it is difficult to move about, for there is a concentration of taverns and cheaper restaurants around the square.

Towering above all is the **Belfort***

*The towering Belfry oversees the Market area, the centre of almost 1 000 years of hustle and bustle.*

(Belfry), some 83m (260ft) high, and claimed to be the finest and largest in all Belgium. It was built in two stages, the two lower storeys in 1282-96, the upper, with the superb lantern, built two centuries later. It is open to the public but you need to be fit to climb it, for there are 366 steps and the higher level is rather claustrophobic. Those who do make it are rewarded with fine **views★★** over the city and beyond. Among the chambers is the treasury, where the city's charters were housed in iron boxes. Another chamber houses the keys of the carillon. The city carilloneur plays music three times a week, in the evening in summer and at noon in winter. The repertoire is wide, ranging from Beethoven to Dixieland jazz, making full use of the 47 bells.

Beneath the Belfry is the massive building

*Hundreds of bicycles congregate around the statue celebrating the Battle of the Golden Spurs, in front of the Palace, home to the Provincial Government.*

called the **Hallen★★★** (Halls), the original market and trading place, built around a courtyard dating from the 13C though restored many times since.

If you stand with your back to the Belfry, on the right is the century-old **Palace** now housing the Provincial Government of West Flanders, of which Bruges is the capital. On the left is the café called Craenenburg. Today it is the epitome of cosy comfort but it has a dark history. It was in a mansion on this site that the husband of Mary of Burgundy, the Austrian governor Maximilian, was confined by an enraged populace while his chancellor was beheaded in the square outside. The statue in the centre is to the heroes of the Battle of the Golden Spurs in 1302, Jan Breydel and Pieter de Coninck together clutching a single sword (*see* p.10).

### Burg★★

Connected to the Markt by Breidelstraat (with several good lace shops), this is the very heart of the medieval city for, as its name implies, it is the site of the fort, built in the 9C, around which the city developed. The fort has long since disappeared and the Burg is now a charming, intimate little square, frequently the venue for evening concerts. It is ringed by architecture ranging from the 12C to the 20C, and the southern side contains Bruges' most important historical buildings.

Although small and tucked away in a corner of the square, the **Heilige Bloed Basiliek★** (Holy Blood Basilica) is one of Flanders' most important churches, for it houses the Reliquary of the Holy Blood, centrepiece of the dramatic annual

**Procession of the Holy Blood★★★**, held on
Ascension Day (*see* p.98)

The basilica is in two parts, with the
**Chapel of St Basil★** in the crypt and the
**Chapel of the Holy Blood** on the first floor.
The crypt is pure Romanesque, unchanged
since it was built in the beginning of the 12C
to house a relic of St Basil, brought from the
Holy Land in 1099. The massive, close-set
columns in the shadowy chamber make it a
deeply evocative place. The only decoration
is in the form of a relief, possibly of the
baptism of St Basil, carved over the doorway
leading into a side aisle. The upper chapel is
reached by a handsome early-16C outdoor

*Once part of a
medieval fort, the
charming square of
Burg is illuminated
against the Belfry.*

staircase. Unlike the crypt, the Chapel of the Holy Blood has been rebuilt on various occasions since the 15C, and was last decorated in a gaudy style in the 19C. According to tradition, the Blood of Jesus Christ was given to a Flemish knight during the Second Crusade, in 1148. It is contained in a rock-crystal phial housed in a magnificent silver reliquary kept in the adjacent museum. The phial is venerated each Friday.

In the centre of the southern side of the Burg is the **Stadhuis** (City Hall), the oldest in Belgium. Built about 1376, its façade dating from the 15C is embellished with

*Heavily gilded statues of knights and angels adorn the façade of Bruges' most revered church, the Holy Blood Basilica.*

*Golden angels holding a coat of arms feature as a carved relief on the Stadhuis.*

statues of the counts and countesses of Flanders. Some were reputed to be the work of Jan van Eyck but all the originals were destroyed by the French in 1792 and these are 19C copies. On the first floor is the superb 14C Gothic Hall, with its neo-Gothic wall paintings and impressive wooden and

*To the left of the Gothic masterpiece of the Stadhuis is the Museum van het Brugse Vrije.*

polychromed vault. (Open daily, 9.30am-5pm, Apr-Sept; daily, 9.30am-12.30pm, 2-5pm, Oct-Mar.)

The **Paleis van het Brugse Vrije** (Palace of the Freemen of Bruges) was the seat of the magistrates of the region, known as Brugse Vrije (Free Bruges). Adjacent is the **Museum van het Brugse Vrije**, whose main interest is the fabulous **chimneypiece★**, made of oak, alabaster and black marble, in the Aldermen's Room. The work of the Bruges artist Lancelot Blondeel (1498-1561), it reflects the complexity of Flemish history, celebrating as it does the defeat of the French king Francois I by the Emperor Charles V at the Battle of Pavia, in Italy. In the centre is the Emperor, who was also Count of Flanders. He is flanked by his grandparents: on the left is Maximilian of

*Resplendent oak carvings depicting the Emperor Charles V and his grandparents adorn the chimneypiece, at the Museum van het Brugse Vrije.*

Austria and Mary of Burgundy, on the right
Ferdinand of Aragon and Isabella of Castile.

Beside the City Hall, the narrow Blinde
Ezelstraat (Blind Donkey Street – probably
named after a local tavern) leads directly
into one of the oldest and most picturesque
parts of Bruges. It is a delight to wander at
random through the tangle of narrow
streets, crossing and re-crossing the ancient
bridges, for each change of direction brings
an entirely new vista. The buildings of the
**Vismarkt** (Fish Market) date only from the
early 19C but have the dignity of Classical
columns, evidence of the Flemish attitude to
trade. Nearby is the **Huidenvettersplein**
(Tanners' Square), with the craft houses of
the tanners, many of which are now cafés
and restaurants.

*The charming canals around Blind Donkey Street are a popular rendevous for tour boats.*

*A humpbacked bridge, a quiet canal, ivy-covered walls, a vaulted window, the far-off trill of carillon bells – in its slumber, Bruges dreams of the time when it was the commercial heart of Europe.*

The much-photographed broad, handsome **Dijver**, flanked on one side by a canal, on the other by gabled houses, is one of the main starting points for **boat tours★★★** along the city's picturesque canals. Lasting 30-40 minutes, the boat tours take in all the main sights from the Begijnhof to Spiegelrei, with several landing stages along the way. An excellent way to get a feel for the layout of the city before exploring on foot, a trip along Bruges' waterways is much more. To view the medieval buildings from the dark waters, alongside the gliding swans, is a magical and unforgettable experience, and one which should be top of the list for all visitors to the city (details of tours can be found on p.96).

## SOUTHERN BRUGES

Beyond the Fish Market, the Dijver leads to another attractive group of buildings set among gardens. This group contains some of the most important museums in Europe, together with Bruges' principal church.

### Groeningemuseum★★★

Allow plenty of time for the Groeninge-museum (also known as the **Stedelijk Museum voor Schone Kunsten**), for it contains what is probably Europe's richest collection of medieval art and provides an excellent overview of Dutch and Belgian art from the 15C to the present day. Among the Flemish Primitives are Hugo van der Goes, Rogier van der Weyden, Gerard David, Petrus Christus and the weird work of Hieronymus Bosch, represented here by *The Last Judgement*. Pride of place is undoubtedly Jan van Eyck's *Madonna with Canon van der Paele*, with the enthroned Madonna flanked by St

Donatian, robed as a bishop, and St George in full armour with the Canon kneeling in front of him. Scarcely less impressive is Gerard David's gruesome *Judgement of Cambyses*, with the corrupt judge being flayed in horrifically accurate detail. (Open daily, 9.30am-5pm, Apr-Sept; daily except Tue, 9.30am-12.30pm, 2-5pm, Oct-Mar.)

*Pride of place in the Groeningemuseum goes to Jan van Eyck's Madonna with Canon van der Paele.*

Further along the Dijver at no 16 is the **Arentshuis★** (Brangwyn Museum). Set in a delightful garden, the museum contains works by the Welsh painter, Sir Frank Brangwyn, who bequeathed them to Bruges, where he was born in 1867. It also includes a collection of lace.

At no 12 is the **Gruuthusemuseum★**, the immense 15C mansion of a family who made their fortune from toll rights on *gruut*, a herb used for brewing beer. The museum

*One of the rooms in the 15C Gruuthuse, home of the family who happily monopolised early beer production.*

contains a wide range of historical artefacts, including a working 18C guillotine.

The towering spire of the great **Onze Lieve Vrouwekerk**★ (Church of Our Lady), is visible for many miles and rivals the Belfry as a symbol of Bruges. Although it is a Gothic building, begun about 1220, the interior is relatively plain. Its major treasure is the **Madonna and Child**★★ by Michelangelo, donated to the church by Bruges citizen Jan van Moescren, shortly after it was sculpted. First it was stolen by Napoleon, then by Herman Goering during the Second World War. Behind the high altar are the splendid tombs of Charles the Bold, Duke of Burgundy, and the magnificent **tomb**★★ of Mary, his daughter, all fine examples of Renaissance carving and richly decorated. Mary died in 1482 at the age of 25 after falling from a horse. Her actual tomb is just visible in the crypt beneath. On the north side of the church you can see the oratory through which the family in the Gruuthuse, physically linked to the church, could follow the services.

Opposite the church is **Sint-Janshospitaal** (St John's Hospital). Housed in the church and adjoining chapel of the complex is the **Memlingmuseum★★★**, which contains six of the Master's most important works. Claimed to be the oldest hospital in Europe, with regulations dating back to 1188 and in use until 1976, the building is mostly early 13C. The 17C apothecary's shop is set out as a museum. Memling's works were intended for the hospital, and so have remained in situ for five centuries. The works include *The Mystical Marriage of St Catherine* and the exquisite *Reliquary of St Ursula*.

Madonna and Child *by Michelangelo, Church of Our Lady.*

Made in the form of a miniature church, the reliquary is decorated with the legend of St Ursula and her 11 000 virgins who were martyred in Cologne. (Open daily, 9.30am-5pm, Apr-Sept; daily except Wed, 9.30am-noon, 2-5pm, Oct-Mar.)

**Oud Sint-Jan** (Old St John's), the 19C development of the hospital, has been turned into a modern visitor centre, with a gallery for exhibitions and an excellent restaurant and quay-side café.

South of St John's Hospital the lively little square of **Wijngaardplein**, with its restaurants and cafés, is an immensely popular tourist attraction. Look for the handsome horse's head which supplies water for the carriage horses. A pretty little bridge leads over the canal to the **Begijnhof★★**

(Beguinage) containing a church and whitewashed houses surrounding a green. Founded in the 13C, it originally housed the Beguines – women not bound by religious vows but who devoted their lives to charitable works. The last of the Beguines died about 50 years ago and the Beguinage is now occupied by Benedictine nuns, who still wear the traditional Beguine habit. The Beguinage is particularly beautiful in the spring, when the golden carpet of daffodils seems to light up the solemn elms. The house near the entrance is furnished as a museum showing the life of the Beguines. Take time to wander through the surrounding unchanged 17C streets.

Leave the Beguinage at the far end and you will find the delightful **Minnewater** (Lake of Love). Despite its romantic name, the origins of the Lake are prosaic, for this was once the harbour of Bruges. It is possible to walk all round it gaining an excellent view of the city from the bridge. The tower is the **Gunpowder Tower**, once used to house ammunition for the Bruges army.

*Romantic surroundings for a light lunch in Wijngaardplein.*

## WESTERN BRUGES

Leading west from the Markt is Steenstraat, lined with gabled guild houses, many topped with gilded symbols. Off Steenstraat, on the left, is the oldest parish church in Bruges, **Sint Salvators-Kathedraal** (St Saviour's Cathedral). Much was rebuilt in the 18C but the 13C choir stalls have survived, together with the impressive Gothic portals. Back on Steenstraat, heading west, you come to the immense square of **'t Zand**, which is not only attractive but an outstanding piece of engineering, for underneath is a car park. The market held every Saturday in the square was transferred here in 1983 from the Markt. The elaborate modern sculpted fountain in the middle is on the site of a 19C railway station.

On the other side of the square, Smedenstraat leads to **Smedenpoort** (Blacksmith's Gate), one of the surviving city gates, built in the 14C. The bronze head replaces the skull of a traitor who opened the Gate to the French in the 15C and was hanged there.

## NORTH-EAST BRUGES

Sometimes called Hanseatic Bruges, this region was settled by foreign merchants, predominantly Venetian, Florentine and Genoese. There are several places of interest in this area.

The **Kantcentrum** (Lace Centre) museum is housed in 15C almshouses, while the workshops are in the former home of a Genoese family, the Adornes. Adjoining is the **Jeruzalemkerk** (Jerusalem Church), built in 1421 also by the Adornes, and still owned by them. It is based probably on the plan of the Holy Sepulchre church in

Jerusalem which two of the Adornes brothers visited on pilgrimage. It contains the tomb of Anselm Adornes and his wife, who became burgomaster of Bruges and was murdered in Scotland in 1484 when acting as consul there.

The **Museum voor Volkskunde★** (Folklore Museum) is also housed in former almshouses, built around a courtyard. It contains reconstructions of traditional interiors, including a cobbler's workshop, a classroom, a kitchen and a shop.

To the north in Carmersstraat is **Schuttersgilde St Sebastiaan**, the longbowmen's guild. Further along the street is **Schuttersgilde St Joris** for the crossbowmen. Both developed into social clubs and are now museums of the crafts.

*Traditional methods can be observed at the working mill of St Janshuismolen.*

**St Janshuismolen** is one of the three surviving windmills on the Vesten, or earthen ramparts. It is still a working mill and can be visited. South of it is the massive **Kruispoort**, another of the four surviving medieval city gates.

### GENT★★★ (GHENT)

The city was founded in the early 7C when two groups of French monks established two abbeys, St Baafs and St Pieters, in an area of marsh and islands (the abbeys still exist today but as museums). By the 10C the wealth of the abbeys attracted the attention of Viking raiders, whose shallow draught vessels could penetrate so far inland. Baldwin of the Iron Arm, Count of Flanders, built a castle to protect the abbeys and the small community that had grown around them, and Ghent came into being as the seat of the Counts of Flanders.

The cloth trade created Ghent's wealth and shaped its history. During the so-called Hundred Years War between France and England (1337-1453), the Counts and upper classes generally favoured the King of France, but the merchants and workers, fearful of losing the supply of English wool vital to their trade, tended to side with the English. In 1338 a merchant, Jacob van Artevelde, made an alliance with Edward III of England. So close was the alliance that Edward's son, John, was born in the city and took his title from it (the English knew him as John of Gaunt).

*The fearsome Gravensteen, 12C castle of the Counts of Flanders, is just as forbidding at night.*

The city experienced to the full the Low Countries' bewildering changes of allegiance as war or dynastic marriages transferred it from one ownership to another, including the Burgundians and the Austrian-Spanish Habsburgs. It suffered particularly badly at the hands of its most famous son, the Emperor Charles V. At first a supporter of the Emperor, the city objected to paying out taxes for his increasingly ambitious military campaigns. Charles crushed the tax revolt with extreme severity, suspending the city's privileges and building a massive castle, at the citizens' expense, to control it.

But whatever glittering dynasty claimed control, the humdrum work of trade and commerce steadily added to the city's wealth. Bruges was its chief rival, the two cities at one stage even going to war against each other. Ghent profited initially when Bruges' main outlet to the sea silted up at the end of the 15C, but in the mid-16C its own clothing trade began to contract in the face of English competition. Resolutely, the merchants developed another trade, exporting grain along the canal which had been dug in 1547, connecting Ghent with the North Sea. The balance of power within the city shifted from the Wool Guild to the Guild of Boatmen.

In the early 19C cloth-making again became important when a merchant, Lieven Bauwens, succeeded in smuggling a spinning jenny from England, together with experienced operatives, and so established Belgium's first cotton mill. In 1822 the canal to Terneuzen was widened and deepened, turning the city into a major commercial port. Ghent felt the full impact of the Industrial Revolution which had passed Bruges by and, though it brought wealth to a small group of society, it polluted the city

with its by-products. The river Leie was ironically known as the Golden River, stained yellow as it was with chemicals. The city is still an important industrial centre but the recognition that tourism has an important economic role to play has led to the restoration and general clean-up of the historic areas. The floodlighting of the major buildings at night turns the historic centre into a spectacular stage-setting.

## EXPLORING THE CITY

Compared with Bruges and Antwerp, Ghent is a sprawling city, without an obvious centre such as Bruges' Markt or Antwerp's Grote Markt. In the late 14C it had the immense population of 50 000 – larger even than Paris – and in consequence its many historic buildings are rather scattered. Orientation is relatively easy, however. Five of the main tram-lines (easy to remember as each has a 1 in its number – 1, 10, 11, 12, 13) run through the city from north to south, ending at the main railway station of St Pieters. Frequent trams, with stops a few hundred yards apart, make it possible to explore at random.

*The inland port of Ghent has replaced trade with 20C tourism, set against the timeless backdrop of guild houses on the Graslei.*

### Must See

**Sint-Baafskathedraal★★** (St Bavo's Cathedral), with van Eyck's **Altarpiece★★★**
Guild houses on the **Graslei★★★**, seen from the Korenlei or from a boat trip on the Leie
**Belfort★★★** (Belfry)
**Museum voor Volkskunde★** (Folklore Museum), on the Kraanlei
**View★★★** from **Sint-Michielsbrug** (St Michael's Bridge)
**Evening stroll** in the historic centre, with many of the buildings illuminated

# EXPLORING GHENT

## THE CENTRE

This circular tour on foot takes about an hour, but you will need to add time if you plan to visit any of the churches and museums along the route.

### Around the Belfort

### Stadhuis (City Hall)

This handsome building was constructed in stages and this is reflected in the contrasting architectural styles of its distinct façades. The oldest part, facing Hoogpoort, was built in 1518-60 in Flamboyant Gothic. The side facing the Botermarkt, though built only 20 years later, is Renaissance in style, while other parts are Baroque and Rococo. It is still the administrative centre for Ghent, so its historic interior can be seen only by guided tours. The magnificent halls on the tour include the Pacificatiezaal, where the Pacification of Ghent was signed in 1576.

*Built over three centuries and encompassing many styles, the Stadhuis represents the changing fortunes of Ghent.*

Opposite, on the Botermarkt, is the **St-Jorishof**, dating from 1478, the former house of the Guild of Crossbowmen, in which both Charles V and Napoleon stayed. It is now a hotel, and lays claim to be the oldest hotel in Europe.

### Belfort★★★ (Belfry)

Built in the mid-14C and heavily restored in the 19C, the Belfry rises to a height of 91m (295ft), and provides splendid **views** over the city. Symbolising the power of the guilds in the Middle Ages, the Belfry is still a landmark in Ghent, being one of the city's great towers. The gilded copper dragon weather-vane dates from 1378. In the public garden to the west stands the great bell, Triomfante, cast in 1660 and taken down because it was cracked. The 52-bell carillon plays each Friday at noon. The vaulted ground floor houses the Information Office. (Belfry open daily, 10am-1.30pm, 2-5pm.)

*The landmark Belfry dwarfs the Cloth Hall in the foreground with St Nicholas' Church tucked away behind.*

Adjoining is the **Lakenhalle** (Cloth Hall), dating from 1425, where the city's wool and cloth traders would meet to buy and sell their goods.

**St Baafsplein**, with the Koninklijke Vlaamse Schouwburg (1891) and the cathedral, was created in the 20C. The low, rather stubby front of the **Sint-Baafskathedraal★★** (St Bavo's Cathedral) does not prepare you for the spacious interior. An extensive period of restoration, still underway, has restored its solemn majesty. The present church was begun about 1290, on the site of a Romanesque church. Only the **crypt★** of the latter (open

*Who could fail to be impressed by the orations delivered from the stunning pulpit in St Bavo's Cathedral?*

to the public) has survived and the rest of the church covers periods from the 13C-16C. It has played a major role in the city's history. In 1445, Philip the Good, Duke of Burgundy, held a Chapter of his recently founded Order of the Golden Fleece here: armorial bearings of the knights are displayed in the south transept. The future Emperor Charles V was christened here. The church is crammed with artistic treasures, including a painting by Rubens in the north transept. A leaflet describing 41 of them is available for a small charge near the entrance. The most prominent feature is the pulpit (1741-45), an extraordinary confection of wood and marble in Flemish Rococo by the sculptor Laurent Delvaux.

*The incomparable masterpiece of the Flemish School – the figures of Adam and Eve among the most poignantly human in all art.*

The supreme treasure of the cathedral is Jan van Eyck's great creation **Het Lam Gods★★★** (*The Lamb of God*, sometimes called *The Mystic Lamb*, or simply the *Ghent Altarpiece*). Painted in 1432, it was intended for the chapel of the donor, Joos Vijd. So meticulous is the work that a jewel on the robe of the foremost singing angel on the left actually reflects a window of the chapel. For security reasons the altarpiece was removed from this chapel in 1986 and is now rather badly housed, in a glass case, in a cramped chamber to the left of the main entrance of the cathedral. An advantage of the new position is that it is possible to view the back of the work. This should not be missed, for it includes a portrait of the donor and his wife (extreme left and right).

The altarpiece consists of 12 oaken panels, eight of which fold to cover the main scene. To left and right are the famous Adam and Eve, outstanding nude portrayals which shocked Emperor Joseph II, who had clothed copies substituted for them. The originals have since been replaced and the copies are on display on pillars by the entrance to the cathedral. The panel on the extreme lower left of the altarpiece is a replacement for one stolen in 1934. Many people are surprised that the central figure being worshipped is a realistic, but ordinary, sheep. It is the symbol of Christ as the Sacrificial Lamb in the Book of Revelation. The far lower left panel shows the Just Judges and the Warriors of Christ, the extreme right shows the Holy Hermits and the Pilgrims, led by a giant St Christopher. In the main scene, four groups of worshippers converge on the Lamb, whose altar stands in a flowery meadow. In the background are the skylines of Flemish cities. The sky itself

looks as clear as the day van Eyck painted it, testimony to his skill with oil paint. The altarpiece has been through many vicissitudes, including being carried off by the Germans in the Second World War.

**St Niklaaskerk★** (St Nicholas' Church)
Like the cathedral, this church was built in the 13C on a Romanesque foundation in what is known as the Scheldt-Gothic style. The tower, completed about 1300, was Ghent's first belfry and is another of the city's landmark towers. Restoration of the church, with its richly embellished interior, began in 1960 and was not completed until the late 1990s.

The west front of the church is on the **Korenmarkt** (Corn Market), Ghent's principal square, insofar as it has one. The main tram-stop is in the square. It is a pleasant, bustling place with its inexpensive restaurants and cafés. Adjoining it on the far side is the **Groentemarkt**, the former fish market and site of the medieval pillory. These restored gabled buildings of the market, guild houses and chapel are interspersed with a collection of cafés and small shops and what is claimed to be Belgium's smallest pub, the ominously named **Galgenhuisje** (Little Gallows House). It is usually open only in the evening, mostly for meals (*see* p.121).

**Graslei to the Stadhuis via the Gravensteen**
**Sint-Michielsbrug** (St Michael's Bridge), leading from the Korenmarkt, provides the most famous **view★★★** in Ghent, with the three giant towers of the Belfort, St Nicholas and St Bavo's in line with each other. The

*Jan van Eyck's Het Lam Gods (The Lamb of God), St Bavo's Cathedral, Ghent.*

*View from St Michael's Bridge, with the three giant towers of the Belfort, St Nicholas and the Cathedral.*

bridge leads to the **Korenlei** (Corn Quay), which provides the best view of the superb guild houses lining the **Graslei★★★** across the stretch of water that was once the old port of the **medieval city★★★**.

The **guild houses** span some 500 years, spectacular buildings each with its emblem bearing testimony to the power of the guilds. Nearest the bridge is the neo-Gothic post office (1906). Immediately adjacent is the Brabantine Gothic **Gildehuis der Vrije Schippers** (Free Boatmen, 1531). Next is the **Gildehuis der Graanmeters** (Grain Measurers, 1698), and beside it the tiny **Tolhuisje** or Little Custom House. The towering gabled front of the **Koornstapelhuis**, where the grain was stored, is pure Romanesque, built about 1200 and the oldest of the group. Next is the **Eeste Korenmetershuis** (15C), representing

*Across the River Leie, the proud houses of trade guilds confront the humble whitewashed buildings of the old hospices – two sides of the river, two sides of the city's past.*

the Guild of the Grain Weighers, and finally the **Gildehuis van de Metselaars**, the Masons' Guild.

Leading out of the Korenlei from the northern end is Jan Breydelstraat, where you will find the **Museum voor Sierkunst en Vormgeving** (Museum of Decorative Arts and Design) which is more interesting than its rather technical title would indicate. It is housed in the 18C mansion of a wealthy family and contains domestic artefacts and furniture from the 17C onwards. Don't miss the extraordinary wooden dining room, tucked away on the ground floor where everything, even the chandelier, is made of exquisitely carved wood. The modern extension to the museum, designed by Willy Verstrachte and opened in 1992, is an attraction in its own right. It contains an important collection of art nouveau artefacts, together with art deco and a contemporary collection.

Immediately opposite the museum you can see the confluence of the rivers Leie and Lieve, while on the far side is the immensely long, low stone hall of the **Groot Vleeshuis** (Butchers' Hall), built in 1404 and now empty while its future is debated. At the end of Jan Breydelstraat you are confronted with the distinctive façade of the **Huis der Gekroonde Hoofden** (Crowned Heads House). The portrait busts that decorate the building are of the Counts of Flanders, the lowest row showing Maximilian, who inherited Flanders through Mary of Burgundy, his son Philip, grandson Charles (later the Emperor Charles V) and Charles's son Philip of Spain.

Gewad, the narrow lane to the right, leads to the area known as **Prinsenhof** (Prince's

Court), whose changing fortunes reflect that of the city's. Charles V was born in the Prinsenhof in 1500. It was demolished in the 17C and the area became an industrial slum. It is now being restored and is fashionable once again. The garden of the palace survives as part of a monastery, together with the building which housed the lions brought by Charles from Africa. A statue was erected to him in 1966 in the little square here. Just beyond this is the Lievekaai, which runs beside the canal dug in the 14C to connect Ghent with Bruges.

Retracing your steps back down Gewad, turn left over the swing bridge and you come to Sint-Veerleplein, where heretics were burned during the days of the Inquisition. It was also home to the **Vismark**

*Portrait busts at each level on the Crowned Heads House depict the successive Counts of Flanders.*

(Fish Market). Although dilapidated now, its splendid 17C entrance gate with stone sculptures symbolising the two rivers indicates its past importance.

Overlooking the square on the confluence of the Leie and the Lieve is the brutal mass of the **Gravensteen★★**, the Castle of the Counts of Flanders, built in 1180. The route through it leads up and down spiral staircases and narrow passages, and is not for the unfit or vertiginous, though children will enjoy following the arrows that mark the route through the passages, chambers and underground dungeons. There is an excellent **view★** of the city from the roof of the keep and the battlement walls. There is also a small **museum** containing horrific instruments of torture. In the Great Hall, in 1339, Edward III of England and his Queen Philippa feasted with Jacob van Artevelde, whilst in 1445 Philip the Good, Duke of Burgundy gave a banquet here for the Knights of the Golden Fleece. The Council of Flanders met in the Audience Chamber of the Counts' Residence for over 300 years. Although rather heavily restored, it provides a vivid example of the grim reality of a medieval castle; the slits from which the crossbows were fired and burning oil was poured are clearly in evidence. Once its military days were over, it served a number of functions. It was used for industrial purposes during the 19C, including providing a machine room for a cotton mill, and has been used as a court, a jail and a mint.

Beyond the square, in an area where the delightful medieval street patterns are almost unchanged, is a narrow lane, the **Kraanlei**, which runs alongside the river. About halfway along is the **Museum voor**

**Volkskunde★** (Folklore Museum),
one of the most enchanting of
Ghent's museums. Allow as much
time as possible for, apart from its
fascinating contents, the buildings
themselves are of great interest.
The main body of the museum
consists of 18 almshouses, built in
1363. The route forms a kind of
maze, for the visitor first proceeds
along the upper floor of the houses
(doorways have been knocked
through the partition walls), then
down along the ground floor,
across to the chapel and finally,
disconcertingly, down through the
crypt of the chapel and out. The
main theme of the museum is a
series of re-constructed interiors –
a grocery, a bedroom, cooperage
and the like – showing daily life in Ghent in
the late 19C. Other rooms are crammed with
exhibits ranging from children's board
games to the two giant figures used in
pageants, housed in the chapel. There is a
puppet theatre, with regular shows, and a
café which at first sight appears to be part of
the exhibits, but serves real refreshments.
(Open Tue-Sun, 9am-12.30pm, 1.30-5.30pm,
Apr-Oct; Tue-Sun, 10am-noon, 1.30-5pm,
Nov-Mar.)

*The Friday Market, whose menagerie of modern bric-a-brac and antiques should appeal to most purse strings.*

Just beyond the museum, at the end of the
Kraanlei, is Temmerman's sweetshop (*see*
p.107), which has a remarkable carved front
showing the Works of Mercy. Look out for
other elaborate shop fronts in this area.
Across the river squats **Dulle Griet** (Mad
Meg), an enormous 15C siege gun named
after the legendary figure who symbolised
violence.

### Vrijdagmarkt (Friday Market)

This immense, empty square comes to life every Friday. The tall turret, the **Toreken**, was part of the Tanners' Guildhouse whose bell sounded the opening of the market. The statue in the centre is of Jacob van Artevelde; his rebellion in 1338 started in the square. Beyond is the massive Romanesque **Sint-Jakobskerk** (St James' Church). The twin towers are 12C but the rest was built over successive centuries. From here, the Belfortstraat leads back to the City Hall and the starting point of the walk.

## EAST OF THE CENTRE

**Sint-Baafsabdij** (St Baafs Abbey) is on the far side of the river Leie, an attractive historic survival set in a garden. Founded in the 7C, it is one of the two abbeys around which Ghent grew, and has witnessed many significant historical events over the centuries. Edward III's queen gave birth to the future John of Gaunt here, and it was here in 1369 that Philip the Bold of Burgundy married Margaret, heiress of Louis de Male, Count of Flanders, and began the Burgundian rule of Flanders. Most of the abbey was demolished by Charles V in 1540 to build his castle, and the remains of the abbey today house a lapidary museum.

Situated on Violettenstraat, on the opposite bank of the Leie, is the **Klein Begijnhof★** (Little Beguinage). Founded in 1234, it was occupied by a few Beguines right up until the 1960s, but most of the houses are now passing into private ownership. Each of them has its own yard, and they are set around a peaceful green. Take time to look into the Baroque chapel.

## SOUTH OF THE CENTRE

There are three important museums in this area. Time and energy can be saved by taking the tram from the Korenmarkt to St Pieters Station as far as Godshuizenlaan.

Godshuizenlaan takes its name from the immense Cistercian abbey of Bijloke, which today houses the **Bijloke Museum★★**. Founded in the early 13C, the surviving buildings in traditional Flemish brick range from the 14C-17C, and are worth visiting in their own right. The entrance is through the 17C portal of the **Groot Begijnhof** (Great Beguinage), placed here in the 19C. There are some 30 rooms in the museum, whose exhibits illustrate the history of Flanders and (in Rooms 28 and 29) Ghent in particular. Room 18 (the old dormitory) contains a display of items relating to the guilds. The exhibits continue on into the cloister and the abbess's house. (Open Mon-Wed, Fri-Sat, 10am-1pm, 2-6pm.)

A few hundred metres south of the Bijloke Museum is **Citadelpark**, with the **Museum voor Schone Kunsten★★** (Fine Arts Museum), situated in a handsome building of 1902 on the edge of the park. The works are those of European masters and cover the period from the 14C to the first half of the 20C. There is a particularly fine collection of Flemish Primitives, including Hieronymus Bosch's *Christ Carrying the Cross* with its nightmarish figures, and work of the School of Van der Goes (open Tue-Sun, 9.30am-5pm). A few yards away in the park is the **Museum van Hedendaagse Kunst** (Museum of Contemporary Art) with its collection of post-war art, including Pop Art.(Renovation work is underway; the main museum is due to open in May or at the end of 1999.)

*Cool, classic lines in the Fine Arts Museum.*

## GETTING AWAY

### The Polders

The best way of seeing this characteristic feature of Flanders is by bicycle. A good starting point is from the pretty little town of **Damme**, about 7km (4.3 miles) from Bruges. Buses depart frequently from Bruges and it is also possible to get there by boat. Bicycles are available for hire near the Stadhuis in Damme and the tourist office in the Stadhuis will provide a map for a bicycle route. The cycle path runs for most of the way along the tops of the dykes, providing wide views over the flat landscape and a relaxing break from the bustle of city sightseeing.

*Whitewashed windmills provide a charming backdrop for cycling excursions to the Polders from Damme, near Bruges.*

## The Seaside

The whole of the coast of Flanders, from De Panne in the south to Knokke 70km (44 miles) away in the north, has been developed as a holiday resort, with Zeebrugge and Ostende doubling as major international ports. A frequent tram service connects all 13 towns along this coastline. The main attraction is, of course, the immensely long sandy beaches, but each town has developed its own tourist facilities.

**Ostende★**, with the remains of a medieval centre, is the most important. It boasts extensive sandy beaches, a promenade and marina, a casino, shopping centre, parks and a number of museums, including a major museum of modern art. Known in Belgium as the 'Queen of seaside resorts', Ostende's appeal lies in its elegant neo-classical buildings and the charm of its past as a fashionable royal summer resort. Today, British day-trippers enjoy its busy seafront, the mussels and French fries, and intensive shopping.

*At last – the beach! Ostende has sandy beaches extending as far as the eye can see.*

The up-market, fashion-conscious visitor will head for the more sophisticated **Knokke-Heist★★**, with its shops, casinos, galleries and events specially geared for tourists. There are lovely walks and cycle-rides in the surrounding dunes and countryside, and those in search of peace, plants and wildlife will enjoy the nature reserve of **Het Zwin★** between Knokke and the Dutch border.

**Blankenberge★** is one of the liveliest resorts, with a casino and plenty of bars, clubs and nightlife.

There are Tourist Offices in Ostende (on Monacoplein ☎ **(059) 70 11 99**); Blankenberge (on the high street ☎ **(050) 41 22 27**); Zeebrugge (on the sea front ☎ **(050) 54 50 42**); De Haan (by the main tram stop ☎ **(059) 24 21 35**); and Knokke (on the Zeedijk ☎ **(050) 63 03 38**).

*There is always plenty of activity in Ostende's colourful harbour.*

## WEATHER

As might be expected, the weather at this north-western tip of Europe is changeable. In general, winters are colder than in southern Britain, averaging 3°C (38°F), and even in summer the north-east wind is noticeable along the coast. Summers can be extremely hot, with temperatures reaching the mid 30s°C (86°F), but average temperatures are usually around a more comfortable 19°C (66°F). However, summer days can be wet and cold, so unless a spell of hot weather is firmly predicted it is as well to have one or two items of warm clothing.

The best time for visiting the cities is between April and October, with July and August being the hottest months. Fine weather in winter or summer will display one of the characteristics of the Flemish landscape which appears again and again in the works of the Old Masters: the enormous skies arching over to meet the distant horizon.

## GETTING ACQUAINTED

Flemings tend to be formal and somewhat reserved on first acquaintance. It is perhaps not surprising that the citizens of a country that has again and again been invaded, has repeatedly seen a different flag flying over official buildings or been obliged to communicate in an alien language, should reserve judgement on a newcomer. Flemings, however, are a people who enjoy life to the full, as is attested by the cafés and bars bursting with young and old into the small hours. Eating and drinking are a vital part of everyday living, and the Flemings indulge heartily and with such great enthusiasm that it is difficult for the visitor not to be drawn in too; you are sure to spend a good few hours of your stay in restaurants and cafés – and why not? It is one place where you can be sure of capturing the real atmosphere of the place.

All three cities pride themselves on the fact that, although they are not crime-free (no city could claim that), crime is kept firmly under control. In Antwerp it is as well to be wary at night in the region north of St Paul's, merging onto the docks. The Sinjoren wryly refer to this as the 'Rosse buurt' or 'warm region' (Red Light district), for the ladies touting their wares in windows wear but the lightest costumes. Likewise, the bars can be rough in the dock area and are best avoided.

## CITY TOURS

It is delightful to ramble at random around all three cities, exploring the medieval streets where at almost every turn a surprise is in store, but a conducted tour provides an overall perspective, particularly if time is limited. The Tourist Offices will provide official guides in all languages for personally tailored tours, but the following are available on a regular basis.

### Antwerp

**Tram tour** of the historic city, lasting about 50 minutes. The tram stop is in the Groenplaats, just outside the Hilton Hotel.
**Flandria** This luxurious cruiser, moored near the Steen, provides a variety of excursions. A round trip on the Scheldt, lasting about 50 minutes, gives an excellent picture of the city

*A romantic boat trip along the canals of Bruges' Blind Donkey area.*

and its relationship to the river. There is a special tour around the enormous port itself, lasting 2½ hours. Evening trips include dinner with wine, lasting about 3 hours, and there are also day trips to tourist destinations. Most tours start from the pontoon near the Steen, where there is also a ticket and information office ☎ (03) 23 31 00 (a Combined Ticket which includes a half-day visit to the Zoo is also available). Tours round the port depart from Kaai 13 Londenbrug, Little Island (a special bus runs to and from Londenbrug-Steen).

**Port** A tour of the Port is possible only by car because of the distances involved. The Tourist Office will provide a route guide which you can follow. They also have a number of themed guided-walk leaflets for sale which will enable you to explore aspects of the city on foot.

## Bruges

**Walking tours** The Tourist Office offers a number of multilingual themed guided walking tours (such as *Maritime Bruges*, *The less-known face of Bruges*, *Bruges the incomparable*, and *The former city ramparts*) each lasting 2 hours (July-Aug, departing at 3pm from the Tourist Office, Burg 11 ☎ (050) 44 86 86).

**Horse-tram tours**, lasting 45 minutes with a stop near the Lake of Love, leave from 't Zand, daily from 10am (Den Oekden Peerdentram ☎ (050) 79 04 37). You can also see Bruges from a horse-drawn cab. The half-hour tour includes a stop at the Beguinage (departs throughout the day from Markt; on Wednesday mornings from Burg).

**Mini-coach tours** with simultaneous translations through individual headphones, lasting 50 minutes, leave hourly from the Burg from 10am (Sightseeing Line ☎ (050) 31 13 55).

**Open-boat tours** of the canals leave from the Dijver and last about 30 minutes (daily, 10am-6pm, Mar-Nov; weekends and on public holidays, Dec-Feb). Book at the Tourist Office or through one of the boat companies: BVBA Venetië van het Noorden ☎ (050) 33 00 41; NV Coudenys ☎ (050) 33 13 75; BVBA Bootexcursies Gruuthuse ☎ (050) 33 32 93; NV STAEL ☎ (050) 33 27 71; F Demeulemeester ☎ (050) 33 41 20.

## Ghent

**Water tours** The city has been steadily linking up its extensive waterways so that eventually it will be possible to travel along them all. The waterways are so important that a separate agency has been set up. For general information and reservations contact: Benelux-Gent-Watertoerist NV, Baarledopstraat 87, 9031 Gent-Drongen ☎ **(09) 282 92 48**. Boats depart from the Graslei for both open and roofed-over sightseeing tours around Ghent (daily 10am-7pm, Apr-Oct; Sat, Sun at 11.30am, Nov-Mar). There are daily boat tours from the Korenlei operated by De Bootjes van Gent, Halve-maanstraat 41, 9040 Gent ☎ **(09) 223 88 53** (daily, every 10 mins from 10am-7pm, Apr-Oct).

**Mini-yachts**, accommodating between 4 and 7 people, can be hired for periods of 2 to 8 hours, or more by special arrangement. The route is on the Leie to St Martens-Latem and Deurle. Necessary instructions and sailing routes are provided (contact Rederij Minerva BVBA, Kareelstraat 6, 9051 Gent ☎ **(09) 221 84 51**).

**Carriage trips**, each of approximately 30 minutes, are an excellent way of getting a quick, overall view of the city. They depart from the Sint-Baafsplein, in front of the Cathedral (daily, 10am-7pm, Apr-Oct).

**Velo-taxis** provide unusual 30-minute tours for two people around the main city sights; contact City Go-Go ☎ **0800 12489**.

**Walking tours** lasting 2 hours depart daily from the Tourist Office at the Belfry, Raadskelder, at 2.30pm (Apr-Nov; Gidsenbond van Gent en Oost-Vlaanderen ☎ **(09) 233 07 72**).

*Be drawn into the past – traditional transport will take you there, 't Zand, Bruges.*

## CALENDAR OF EVENTS

In addition to the tourist attractions, Flanders has a wide range of events and festivals which should help you get a real flavour of Flemish life and culture – processions, parades, folk events, music festivals, concerts and ballet performances, exhibitions, fairs and special markets. The annual **Festival of Flanders** runs from April to October, and its international-flavour programme of events, held in a variety of venues in the major cities, is sure to include something of interest.

The region also has a rich tradition of folklore festivals, the origins of which are not always clear today but which provide a colourful and fun way for locals and visitors to let their hair down. The pre-Lenten Carnival week is the main time for processions of floats, costumed marchers, traditional foods and uninhibited revelry, but there are so many events during the year that you are sure to find something to coincide with your visit. Below we give a guide to some of the more important festivals and events in Bruges, Antwerp and Ghent, but call in at the local Tourist Office to check what is on; they publish an events calendar and can help with booking tickets.

### February

Pre-Lenten *carnival* celebrations throughout the region. In Antwerp, the celebrations begin with traditional *Sword Dancing* by the Lange Wapper dance company, and culminate in March with the *Procession of the Processions*.

### March

**Ghent** *Flanders Spring Fair* (Flanders Expo).

### May

**Ghent** *International Jazz festival*, held over two days (Eurotent, Braemkasteelstraat).

**Bruges** *Procession of the Holy Blood*: this Ascension Day parade, dating back 800 years, is Bruges' most famous event. Thousands dress in medieval costumes, portraying scenes from the Bible, and a relic of the Holy Blood is carried through the streets.

### June

*Dag van de Beiaard* (Day of the Carillon): around the third week of the month, all carilloneurs sound out in the cities and towns across Flanders.

### July

**Ghent** *Gentse Feesten*: a week of popular cultural festivities, held in the city centre, including music and street theatre, street animation, balls and fireworks. In the *Tour of the Guild of Ropes* (3rd week in July), a barefoot group dressed in tabards, with a rope around their necks, walk around the town re-enacting the penitential trip of 1540.

**Antwerp** *Summer of Antwerp*: lasting through to August, events are staged in the city centre in this annual festival.

**Bruges** *Cactus Festival*: three-day open-air music festival (pop, blues, reggae, afro), held in Minnewater park.

## August

**Bruges** *Festival of the Canals*: night-time pageant staged along the illuminated city canals.

**Bruges** *Pageant of the Golden Tree*: five-yearly commemoration of the wedding of Charles the Bold and Margaret of York (next to be held in 2000).

**Antwerp** *Rubensmarkt* (15 August): colourful annual market in which the stall-holders wear costumes from the Rubens era.

**Ghent** *Patersholfeesten*: three days of traditional festivities held in the historic quarter of Het Patershol.

## December

*Kerstmarkten*: traditional Christmas markets, held in Bruges, Antwerp and Ghent.

## May-October 2001

**Antwerp Fashion** For these six months, Antwerp will be holding the largest fashion happening staged in Belgium, with various events and exhibitions held in locations around the city. Contact the tourist information office for further details of specific events.

*Procession of the Holy Blood, Bruges.*

## ACCOMMODATION

Good town planning has meant that very large modern hotels have been introduced into the historic centres of the cities without detriment to their surroundings. The Hilton Hotel in Antwerp, on the Groenplaats, has adapted an existing large department store, but the Sofitel in Ghent is a new building, although opposite the ancient Stadhuis, while the basement of the Holiday Inn in Bruges houses ruins of the long-vanished Burg.

There is a wide choice of accommodation available in Flanders, ranging from the luxurious to the simple, with standards comparable with what you would expect in other major European cities. The majority of hotels are fairly small, atmospheric, often well located and reasonably priced. The absence of large hotels means that you are advised to reserve in advance. Rooms can be booked through Belgium Tourist Reservations, Anspachlaan 111, 1000 Brussels ☎ **(02) 513 74 84**, or through the Tourist Information Offices in each city. A brochure listing accommodation in Flanders can be obtained from Tourism Flanders-Brussels, 31 Pepper Street, London E14 9RW ☎ **0891 88 77 99**.

The Michelin *Red Guide Benelux* lists accommodation

*A department store is now the Hilton Hotel in Groenplaats, Antwerp.*

and restaurants in Bruges, Antwerp and Ghent, together with other towns in Belgium for visitors who wish to make overnight stops or to explore the surrounding areas.

The Benelux classification of five classes of **hotels** and unclassified **guesthouses** means that the potential visitor has a very clear idea of what standards to expect. Within each class every hotel is described through symbols ranging from whether dogs are allowed to the provision of children's cots. Five-star is 'luxury' (there is only one hotel in this category in Flanders – Park Lane Hotel in Antwerp). Four-star is 'first class', with the highest standards of comfort, amenities and service; three-star is 'very good'; two-star is 'average', with bath and wc in at least 25% of all bedrooms; and one-star is described as 'plain', with washstands. Class H hotels offer the most basic facilities.

The following prices are a rough guide to what you can expect to pay for a double room, per night, with breakfast (prices always include VAT and service):

5 star: 5 000–9 000BF
4 star: 3 600–8 000BF
3 star: 2 900–4 000BF
2 star: 2 000–3 800BF
1 star: 1 300–2 500BF

**Bed and breakfast** accommodation is also available; for a list of addresses contact Taxistop, Onderbergen 51, 9000 Gent ☎ **(09) 223 23 10**. Details of the **youth hostels** in Bruges, Antwerp and Ghent can be obtained from: Vlaamse Jeugdherbergcentrale, Van Stralenstraat 40, 2060 Antwerpen ☎ **(03) 232 72 18** (details of some are given below). Lists of inexpensive accommodation for students and budget travellers is also listed in the brochure, *Budget Holidays Flanders*, available from the Tourist Office.

## Recommendations

The list below includes a selection in each of the three cities.

### Antwerp

\*\*\*\* **Firean** *Karel Oomsstraat 6, 2018 Antwerpen* ☎ **(03) 237 02 60**. Stylish mansion, with authentic art deco interior.

\*\*\*\***Hilton** *Groenplaats, 2000 Antwerpen* ☎ **(03) 204 1212**. Well situated in the heart of the historic part of the city.

\*\*\* **Industrie** *Emiel Banningstraat 52, 2000 Antwerpen* ☎ **(03) 238 86 88**. Friendly, personal service in this beautifully restored mansion.

\* **Cammerpoorte** *Nationalestraat 38-40, 2060 Antwerpen* ☎ **(03) 231 97 36**. A friendly, budget hotel in the heart of Antwerp.

\* **Rubenshof** *Amerikalei 115-117, 2000 Antwerpen* ☎ **(03) 237 07 89**. Small, family-run hotel housed in a former cardinal's residence, with authentic atmosphere and Jugendsil architecture.

**Jeugdherberg** (Youth Hostel) in suburbs: *Op-Sinjoorke, Eric Sasselaan 2, 2020 Antwerpen* ☎ **(03) 238 02 73**.

## Bruges

\*\*\*\* **Relais Oud Huis Amsterdam** *Spiegelrei 3, 8000 Brugge* ☎ **(050) 34 18 10**. Situated next to the picturesque canal, tranquil yet close to the centre. The converted 17C mansions have created a unique hotel with individual rooms.

\*\*\*\* **Jan Brito** *Feren Fonteinstraat 1, 8000 Brugge* ☎ **(050) 33 06 52**. This peacefully situated luxury hotel, in a protected 16C monument, has original decorations from the 16C and 17C.

\*\*\* **Ter Duinen** *Langerei 52, 8000 Brugge* ☎ **(050) 33 04 37**. An excellent, quiet hotel overlooking one of Bruges' most beautiful canals.

\*\*\* **Grand Hotel du Sablon** *Noordzandstraat 21, 8000 Brugge* ☎ **(050) 33 39 02**. In the heart of the city, combining tradition with modern comforts.

\* **Leopold** *'t Zand 26, 8000 Brugge* ☎ **(050) 33 51 29**. Small family hotel; summer terrace

overlooking the square.

**Jeugdherberg** (Youth Hostels) *Europa, Baron Ruzettelaan 143, 8310 Assebroek, Brugge* ☎ **(050) 35 26 79**.

*Passage, Dwcerstraat 26, 8000 Brugge* ☎ **(050) 34 02 32** Situated near the Markt; popular with young people. Downstairs is the **Gran Kaffee de Passage**, a lively, informal place for an evening meal.

## Ghent

\*\*\*\* **Sofitel Belfort** *Hoogpoort 63, 9000 Gent* ☎ **(09) 233 33 31**. Stylish and friendly hotel situated in the heart of the historic centre, by the Belfort.

\*\*\* **Aparthotel Castelnou** *Kasteellaan 51, 9000 Gent* ☎ **(09) 235 04 11**. Apartment-style accommodation with full service; central location.

\*\*\* **Ibis Kathedraal** *Limburgstraat 2, 9000 Gent* ☎ **(09) 233 00 00**. Very well situated on St Baafsplein, with views of the cathedral, square and theatre.

\* **Trianon II** *Voskenslaan 36, 9000 Gent* ☎ **(09) 220 48 40**. Stylish and modern rooms at reasonable prices, but located outside the centre near the railway station.

**Jeugdherberg** (Youth Hostel) in city centre: *De Draecke, St Widostraat 11, 9000 Gent* ☎ **(09) 233 70 50**.

## FOOD AND DRINK

Food is an important element in the lifestyle of the Belgians, so you can be assured that you will eat well. Flemings claim that their cuisine has the quality of French and the quantity of German cuisine – and helpings certainly are generous. While the quality is usually very high, food in general is rather expensive. Belgian cuisine follows the linguistic divide – that of the Walloon region is similar to French, while Flanders has its own variety in which fish and seafood play a key role.

Flemings are a hardy race, much addicted to eating outdoors. Even in winter, terrace cafés will be in use, with discreetly placed heaters combating the weather. Only really severe weather will deter clients and, the moment it clears, the tables will be invitingly prepared. The very flexible restaurant hours make it possible to avoid the crowds by eating early or late.

Mussels are virtually a staple, with some restaurants serving nothing else. The dish is served in a variety of ways, including simply steamed, curried or with white wine. Mussels are not particularly cheap, but are sustaining, for they are invariably accompanied by a massive helping of *frites*. A curious etiquette attends its serving. It is perfectly acceptable to drink the delicious broth in which the mussels are cooked – but no spoon is provided. The trick is to ladle up the broth with a mussel shell.

Horsemeat, at which British and American visitors tend to look askance, is in fact a delicacy – tender and sweet and served like beef. A regional dish is *waterzooi*, a kind of stew which changes its ingredients and presentation according to locality: in Antwerp it is composed of shellfish with a minimum of liquid, in Bruges fish is popular,

*Sampling the delights of typical Belgian cuisine.*

while Ghent goes in for chicken in broth. Another dish to try is *karbonaden*, a substantial stew of braised beef or sometimes pork with beer and onions.

Those with room for more after a hearty main course could try one of the 300 or so Belgian cheeses, with many little-known flavours to sample alongside the more famous Gouda and Remoudou.

Belgians have a sweet tooth (as the mouth-watering displays of chocolates and pralines will testify), and desserts usually involve chocolate and cream. There is a huge variety of cakes and pastries; *Lierse Vlaaikens* are tasty plum tarts, while *speculaas* are usually eaten with coffee. Pancakes are popular, and Belgian waffles (*gaufres*) are sold on pavement stalls.

## Drink
**Beer** is to Belgium what wine is to France. Even a modest establishment will offer a choice of a dozen or so of the reputed 600 different kinds of beer. Each is served in its own special glass, the oddest being the *Kwak* served in a glass globe supported by a wooden frame.

A good way to penetrate the mysteries of Belgian beer is to take part in one of the guided tours of the breweries, such as the Huisbrouwerij Straffe Hendrik, in the Walplein, in Bruges. The modest fee includes a glass of the famous Straffe Hendrik, which lives up to its name of 'Strong Henry'.

Popular throughout West Flanders is the dark-red Roden-bach and the gueuzes, the latter include fruit-flavoured beers called Kriek. The group of beers made by monks (among them Trappist and West-vleteren) ferment in the bottle and come in two strengths: the dark-coloured double and the blonde triple.

Belgium shares with its neighbour, the Netherlands, a liking for *geneva*, a juniper-flavoured liquor not so strong as gin and very pleasant to taste. There are more than 270 brands to choose from, each with its own distinctive flavour.

## Recommendations
The suggestions for eating out below are indicated (M) for moderate – a good place for a quick lunch – or (E) for expensive, where you can sample some of the truly remarkable dishes for dinner. The tradition of the tavern still flourishes in Flanders, and most bars will serve hot food ranging from a bowl of soup to a three-course meal.

### Antwerp
**De Foyer** (M) Actually the stunning foyer of the restored

19C Bourla Theatre in the Komedieplaats. There is a buffet with a wide choice of hot and cold food.

**'t Paters Vaetje** (M) A traditional tavern near the Cathedral, with 100 different beers.

**De Gulden Beer** (E) *Grote Markt 14* Good for Italian lunches.

**Rooden Hoed** (E) *Oude Koornmarkt 25* Authentic atmosphere.

**In de Schaduw van den Kathedraal** (E) *Handschoenmarkt 17* Authentic atmosphere, in the historic part of the city.

**'t Lammeke** (E) *Lange Lobroekstraat 51* Typical restaurant in the city centre.

**Neuze Neuze** (E) *Wijngaardstraat 19* Authentic atmosphere.

**De Peerdestal** (E) *Wijngaardstraat 8 (near Grote Markt)*. An attractive tourist restaurant specialising in horsemeat but with a choice of other dishes.

**Dock's Café** (E) *Jordaenskaai 7* Trendily converted maritime warehouse on the river front, specialising in fish.

**Transat** (E) *St Pietersvliet 3* Improbably situated on the 10th floor of an office block, this restaurant provides a spectacular view of the city and the docks. *Waterzooi* is a speciality.

## Bruges

**Huyze Die Maene** (M) *Markt 17* Good bar-restaurant.

**Den Dijver** (M) *Dijver 5* Food and beer; next to the museum.

**De Snippe** (E) *Huysentruyt* Set in an 18C house, with decorative murals and shaded terrace.

**'t Bourgoensche Cruyce** (E) *Wollestraat 41* Delightful setting next to the canal.

**Cafeedraal** (E) *Zilverstraat 38* In a historic building, with a pleasant terrace courtyard.

## Ghent

**Waterzooi** (E) *St-Veerleplein 2* Attractively situated opposite the Castle.

**Het Cooremetershuys** (E) *Graslei 12* Set in a 17C mansion.

**De Blauwe Zalm** (E) *Vrouwebroersstraat 2* In the historic Patershol district; serves traditional seafood dishes.

**Grade** (E) *Charles de Kerchovelaan 81* A modern brasserie.

**Pakhuis** (E) A converted warehouse just off Predikherenlei. There is a wide range of restaurants in Ghent. For a good dinner (most do not open for lunch) in a pleasant atmosphere, try the **Patershol** area, where there is something for everyone, from exotic menus at the **Vier Tafels** (*Plotersgracht 6*), to French cuisine at the **Petit Restaurant** (*Rodekoningstraat 12*). For a slightly less expensive Turkish meal, go to **Sleepstraat** or **Oudburg** nearby. For local specialities try the **Graaf van Egmond** (*Sint-Michielsplein 21*), which also boasts a superb view of the Graslei.

# Lace

A characteristic feature of 17C Flemish portraiture is the delicate lace which edges the necklines and cuffs of both men's and women's clothes – of cut-throat soldiers as well as urban fops. The making of lace (*dentelle* in French, *kant* in Dutch) developed from the 16C onwards. By this time, the wool trade had declined in the face of English competition, and linen production, made from home-grown flax, increased. It was discovered that the fine, but strong, threads of linen were ideal for lace-making.

Over the following centuries, three methods of production developed, first as a form of embroidery, then as needlepoint which used a framework of threads to which loops were attached. Finally, the method which is still used today was developed, using bobbins which are braided and crossed around pins – a delicate and highly skilled

process. Until the 19C, lace-making was done entirely by hand and crossed the social divide, with working-class women producing it as a cottage industry and the upper classes as a socially accepted recreation. From the 19C onwards, machine-made lace using cheaper cotton dominated the market, but hand-made lace of linen or silk is still widely produced, though naturally more expensive. The Lace Centre on the Groenplaats, in Antwerp, has a wide range of the traditional work for sale. In Bruges, the Kantcentrum near the Jerusalem Church (*see* p.72) has workshops where you can watch the fascinating process, as well as a museum where the history of lace-making is displayed (open Mon-Fri, 10am-noon, 2-6pm; Sat, 10am-noon, 2-5pm; demonstrations in afternoons).

*Left: Lace shops display myriads of patterns.*
*Above: The intricacy of the designs can be breathtaking.*
*Top: The delicate tradition lives on.*

## SHOPPING

Note that non-EU visitors are entitled to reclaim VAT. Shops displaying a 'Tax-free for Tourists' logo will supply a shopping cheque which will have to be validated by customs when you leave the country.

### Antwerp

Leading from the historic centre is the broad, traffic-free Meir, where you will find large department stores and international chains, together with trendy boutiques and top fashion houses which spill over into Frankrijklei. Meir leads into that other main shopping street, De Keyserlei, running off which is Quellinstraat with its cinemas, boutiques and travel agencies. Tucked away in galleries in the area are haute-couture shops, with most of the famous names represented.

For **diamonds**, the inexperienced cannot do better than visit Diamondland, on Appelmansstraat, in the diamond quarter near the Centraal

*Tempting hand-fashioned sweets in Temmerman's sweetshop.*

Station, where you will receive expert but impartial advice. Shops selling the world-famous Belgian **chocolates** are everywhere, but Burie's, in Gasthuisstraat 3, impresses even the Sinjoren with their displays of original confections.

## Bruges

Bruges is a shoppers' delight, for in its network of small streets you will discover small shops specialising in items such as lace or chocolates, while other streets, such as Steenstraat, have the chain stores and larger shops where you can buy almost anything. A popular shopping street with high-class shops is St Amandsstraat. Cheaper shops will be found in and around 't Zand.

You will find **lace** almost everywhere in Bruges. Although hand-made lace is expensive, the quality is excellent, but beware of imitations. Gift shops in Breidelstraat, between the Burg and the Markt, specialise in lace. For demonstrations and greater choice try the Kantcentrum (Lace Centre, *see* p.72), or Kantjuweeltje (Lace Jewel) in Philipstockstraat 11, just off the Markt.

## Ghent

The Veldstraat is the main shopping street, with a number of fashion shops and a good bookshop at no 88. Although pedestrianised, trams still run along the street, so you need to take care. There are small specialist shops tucked away in the streets and alleys leading off Veldstraat. The Brabantdam and Volderstraat are the fashion high-spots.

**Sweets** – for a special treat, try Temmerman's, at Kraanlei 79, the sweetshop of every child's dreams, with a dazzling display of home-made sweets in a historic building. Locals make a point of patronising Tierenteyn, on the Groentenmarkt, for **mustard** – expensive, but unique.

## Markets

Open-air markets flourish in Flanders, many of them in the same street or square they have occupied for centuries, and still held on the same day of the week. Many of them are on Sundays, and most are over by midday or a little after. They are also good places to pick up a cheap, hot, snack lunch.

### Antwerp

**Vrijdagmarkt** (Friday Market) Held on Wednesday and Friday in the square of the same name, this specialises in auctions of second-hand goods.
**Vogelmarkt** (Bird Market) Held

on Sundays in the Theater-plein, when birds and animals feature as part of a general market. On Saturday, a range of exotic foods are available.

**Antique Market** Every Saturday on the Handschoenmarkt.

**Rubens Market** Held annually on 15 August on the Grote Markt. Stall-holders sell their wares dressed in period costumes, while traditional entertainers perform.

### Bruges

The main market is held each Saturday on 't Zand. There is a flea market on Saturdays and Sundays on the Dijver.

### Ghent

**Vrijdagmarkt** Flower market held on Saturday and Sunday; bird market on Sunday.

**St-Jacobs** Art and antiques market on Friday, Saturday and Sunday.

**St Michielsplein** Food market on Sunday.

Every Sunday morning a conducted tour leaves the Groentenmarkt at 10am and visits various markets: Kunstmarkt (art market), Blomenmarkt (flower market), Vogelmarkt (bird market), Prondelmarkt (flea market).

## ENTERTAINMENT AND NIGHTLIFE

There are regular music festivals and concerts throughout all three cities during the year, and concerts of classical music, often free, take place in many churches in the evenings. The Tourist Offices publish details.

### Antwerp

Antwerp has a long tradition of **music** and **theatre**, with a number of delightful theatres. **Bourlaschouwburg** (Bourla Theatre, *Komedieplaats 18* ☎ **(03) 231 07 50**) was built in 1829 when it was known as the French Opera House. Housed in historic buildings, the **Koninklijke Vlaamse Opera** (Royal Flemish Opera House, *Frankrijklei 3* ☎ **(03) 233 66 85**) has performances of opera and also the Royal Flanders Ballet. Another gem of a building is **deSingel** (*Desguinlei 25* ☎ **(03) 248 38 00**), a multi-arts centre where you can see opera, concerts, theatre and ballet. The city has more than 20 other theatres and concert halls, providing the full range of music, dance and theatre.

At night, there are several lively areas, notably around the Cathedral (Handschoenmarkt, Oude Korenmarkt); Grand-Place (Hoogstraat, Grote Pieter Potstraat); the quays (Vlaamse Kaai, Jordaenskaai); and around Hendrik Conscience-plain (Wijngaardstraat).

**Jazz** and **folk music** feature at

many of the smaller venues and specialist bars and cafés. The Hoogstraat is also a lively area: look out for the **Café Beveren** on the corner of 't Zand.

## Bruges

Free copies of the monthly 'what's on' magazine, *Exit*, are available at the Tourist Office. The Tourist Office publishes a useful leaflet entitled *Bruges by Night*, detailing attractions. Bruges' nightlife is the quietest of the three cities. A memorable experience is to walk through the silent city at night, when only a handful of major buildings are floodlit and the canals reflect them like mirrors of black glass.

*Brugge Anno 1468* is a **historical banquet**, based on the wedding party of Charles the Bold and Margaret of York (*see* p.55), held in the former Jesuit church. It includes a four-course dinner with wine, and entertainment (every Sat 7.30-10.30pm; booking essential ☎ (050) 34 75 72).

## Ghent

For **opera**, the place to go in Ghent is **De Vlaamse Opera** (*Schouwburgstraat 3* ☎ (09) 225 24 25). At the **Koninklijke Nederlandse Schouwburg** (Royal Dutch Theatre, *St Baafsplein* ☎ (09) 225 32 08) the Dutch Theatrical Company of Ghent put on productions with simultaneous English and French translations.

**Historical banquets** take place in a number of historic buildings, including a 13C monastery, a medieval crypt, the great hall of a castle or in one of Ghent's numerous ancient halls. There is a choice of four menus. Check at the Tourist Office for details.

**Discos** and **nightclubs** are mostly found in the Zuid Quarter, but there is a lot of activity in the Three Towers region. The **Lazy River Jazzclub** (*Stadhuissteeg 5*) has live jazz on Friday nights, while the **Dambord Jazzcafé** (*Korenmarkt 19*) has jazz concerts on Tuesdays. Those looking for international or Irish traditional music should try **Foley's Irish Pub** (*Recolettenlei 10*).

There are several cafés worth checking out. The **Rococo** (*Corduwanierstraat 57*) is a romantic, candlelit spot, while the **'t Velootje** (*Vrijdagmarkt 50*), also in the Patershol, is worth a visit. For a range of beers, try **De Dulle Griet** (*Vrijdagmarkt 50*), while the **Dreupelkot** (*Groentenmarkt 12*) is renowned for its relaxed atmosphere. Ghent's large student population is evident in Overpoortstraat, near St-Pietersplein.

## THE BASICS

### Before You Go

Visitors from the UK and other EU countries entering Belgium should have a full passport (valid for the period in which they will be travelling) or a valid visitor's card for stays of up to 90 days. No visa is required for members of EU countries. Citizens of the Republic of Ireland, the US, Canada, Australia and New Zealand will need a valid passport and can stay for up to three months without a visa. A visa is required for all other countries outside the EU. No vaccinations are necessary.

### Getting There

**By Train:** Rail travel is the ideal means of travelling to Flanders from the UK and within Europe, for Belgian trains are frequent, fast and punctual. **Eurostar** runs 11 services a day, at roughly two-hourly intervals, between London Waterloo and Brussels Midi (Zuid), taking 2 hours 40 minutes. There is little difference between first and standard accommodation, but a meal is included with the first-class fare. It is possible to change at Lille for Bruges but it is a slow journey and it is best to go on to Brussels. Booking a week in advance substantially reduces fares, as does an overnight stay including Saturday. The onward journey time from Brussels to Antwerp and Ghent is around 40 minutes, and about 50 minutes to Bruges. You can book the onward part of your journey with Eurostar. For bookings and enquiries ☎ **0870 6000 715**, or book through your local travel agent or train station.

For information on train schedules and prices in Belgium, contact NMBS (Belgian Rail) in London ☎ **(020) 7593 2332**, or in Bruges ☎ **(050) 38 23 82**, or Antwerp ☎ **(03) 204 20 40**.
**By Air:** Flights from London, various European cities and many US cities fly into the regional airport of Deurne, 5km (3 miles) from the centre of Antwerp ☎ **(03) 218 12 47**. Bruges is about 1 hour away by car or train, and Ghent about 40 minutes.

Belgium's national airport is at Zaventem, 14km (9 miles) outside Brussels. Sabena (Belgian World Airlines) operate to most destinations ☎ **(02) 723 23 23**. Antwerp is 50km (31 miles) away, connected by the E19 autoroute; Bruges is 100km (62 miles) north-west on the E40; Ghent is 50km (31 miles) north-west on the E40. To reach the cities by train from Zaventum you will first need to take a train to Brussels (20 minutes) for connections to Bruges, Antwerp or Ghent.

**By Sea:** There are various options for visitors crossing the Channel by boat. P & O European Ferries operate between Dover and Calais (approximately 75 minutes), while the overnight P & O North Sea Ferries cross between Hull and Zeebrugge (approximately 14 hours) ☎ (01482) 79 51 41. Holyman Sally Ferries sail between Dover and Ostende, with ferries taking about 4 hours while the new catamaran service takes just 1 hour 40 minutes. In summer, Hoverspeed operates Seacat, a 2-hour crossing between Dover and Ostend, for passengers and cars. For more information

☎ 08705 240 241.

**By Car:** If you are taking your car you can either take one of the above ferry crossings, or a quicker option is the **Le Shuttle** drive-on train service between Folkestone and Calais. Using the Channel Tunnel, this frequent service takes just 35 minutes. There is a good network of autoroutes connecting the main cities in Belgium. From Calais, the E40 takes you to Bruges and on to Ghent. From Ghent, the E17 goes north-east to Antwerp.

**By Coach:** Numerous coach companies run services between London and the cities of Flanders. Express Coach operate a service between Lille and Bruges, connecting with the Eurostar and TGV trains ☎ (050) 32 01 11.

*Tours of the Polders take a leisurely look at the landscape.*

# A-Z

## Accidents and Breakdowns

Contact the rental firm in the event of an accident or break-down. If you have an accident, exchange names, addresses and insurance details but on no account move the vehicle, even if you are causing a hold up, as this may affect your insurance claim. In the event of an accident call the emergency number ☎ 100.
For police ☎ 101. *See also* **Driving** and **Emergencies**

## Accommodation see p.100

## Airports see p.112

## Banks

Banks are open 9am-4pm, Mon-Fri, though some close for an hour at lunchtime. A passport is required if you are changing money. Automated teller machines (ATMs) can be found in the main towns and cities. There is a standard com-mission for changing travellers' cheques and foreign currency, but you should always check the rate of exchange being offered. Gen-erally, bureaux de change offer the best rates, followed by banks. Travellers' cheques and cash can also be changed at most hotels, although the exchange rate may not be very favourable. *See also* **Money**

## Bicycles

With such a flat landscape, bicycles are the obvious choice to explore the countryside of the Polders, and are also an easier way of getting around the narrow streets of the cities than cars. **Bruges**, in particular, is a city where cyclists are at a clear advantage – they are even permitted to cycle in both directions down one-way streets. An increasing number of hotels have bicycles for their clients' use, and there are a number of outlets which hire them. You can hire one from the main railway station (☎ 38 58 71) or companies such as 't Koffieboontje, Hallestraat 4 (☎ 33 80 27); Eric Popelier,

Hallestraat 14 (☎ **34 32 62**)
and De Ketting, Gentpoort-
straat 23 (☎ **34 41 96**). Other
suggestions can be obtained
from the Tourist Office. In
**Ghent** you can also hire bikes
from the train station
(St Pieters ☎ **241 22 23**) or
from a hire company such as
Het Verzet, Herman Janssens,
Beekstraat 84 (☎ **380 27 20**).
Bicycle-hire in **Antwerp** is not
as common as in the other
cities – ask at the Tourist Office
for further information.

## Breakdowns see **Accidents**

## Camping
Flanders has a number of well-
equipped campsites
throughout the region, with
some of them being conve-
niently located close to the
historical cities, enabling you
to combine sightseeing in the
city with exploring the countryside. All official campsites
are classified with a star rating
according to the facilities they
offer. The Belgian Tourist
Office has a brochure listing all
the campsites in the region.

## Car Hire
Bruges, Anterp and Gent all
have numerous international
and local car-hire agencies, as
do the airports at Brussels and
Antwerp. Accidents are

frequent so you are strongly
advised to take out collision
damage waiver. If you require a
car with automatic transmis-
sion you should specify this
when booking.

Most companies restrict hire
of cars to drivers over 25 and
under 70. Drivers must have
held a full licence for at least a
year. Unless paying by credit
card, a substantial cash deposit
is required. *See also* **Driving** and
**Accidents and Breakdowns**

## Climate see p.94

## Clothing
The weather can be unpre-
dictable at all times of year, so
you should always be prepared
for rain, even during the
summer months. Spring can be
very pleasant, with bright
sunny days, but the wind can
be chill, as can the evenings, so
it is advisable to wear several
layers that you can take off or
put on as necessary.

Casual wear is generally
acceptable, although smarter
clothing will not be out of
place at 5-star hotels and more
exclusive restaurants.
Remember to dress respect-
fully when visiting churches.

Most clothing measurements
are standard throughout
Europe but differ from those
in the UK and the US. The

following are examples:

## Women's sizes

| UK | 8 | 10 | 12 | 14 | 16 | 18 |
|----|---|----|----|----|----|----|
| Europe | 38 | 40 | 42 | 44 | 46 | 48 |
| US | 6 | 8 | 10 | 12 | 14 | 16 |

## Women's shoes

| UK | 4.5 | 5 | 5.5 | 6 | 6.5 | 7 |
|----|-----|---|-----|---|-----|---|
| Europe | 38 | 38 | 39 | 39 | 40 | 41 |
| US | 6 | 6.5 | 7 | 7.5 | 8 | 8.5 |

## Men's suits

| UK/US | 36 | 38 | 40 | 42 | 44 | 46 |
|-------|----|----|----|----|----|----|
| Europe | 46 | 48 | 50 | 52 | 54 | 56 |

## Men's shirts

| UK/US | 14 | 14.5 | 15 | 15.5 | 16 | 16.5 | 17 |
|-------|----|------|----|------|----|------|----|
| Europe | 36 | 37 | 38 | 39/40 | 41 | 42 | 43 |

## Men's shoes

| UK | 7 | 7.5 | 8.5 | 9.5 | 10.5 | 11 |
|----|---|-----|-----|-----|------|----|
| Europe | 41 | 42 | 43 | 44 | 45 | 46 |
| US | 8 | 8.5 | 9.5 | 10.5 | 11.5 | 12 |

*A contemporary street artist entertains outside the Cathedral of Our Lady, Antwerp.*

## Consulates and Embassies

These are all in Brussels.

**Australia**
Rue Guimard 6, 1040 Brussels
☎ (02) 231 0500

**Canada**
Avenue de Tervuren 2, 1040
Brussels ☎ (02) 735 6040

**Republic of Ireland**
Rue de Luxembourg 19-21,
1040 Brussels ☎ (02) 513 6633

**New Zealand**
Boulevard de Regent 47-48,
1000 Brussels ☎ (02) 512 1040

**UK**
Rue Arlon 85, 1040 Brussels
☎ (02) 287 6211

**US**
Boulevard du Regent 27, 1000
Brussels ☎ (02) 513 3830

## Crime

There is no need to be unduly concerned about crime in any of the cities. All three cities pride themselves on the fact that while they are not crime-free, crime is kept firmly under control. The streets of Bruges, with its large number of tourists, are generally safe, even for women at night. In Antwerp you should avoid the region north of St Paul's, adjoining the docks, which is the Red Light district. Similarly, in Ghent steer clear of the Red Light district between Keizer Karelstraat and Vlaanderenstraat.

It is advisable to take sensible precautions and be on your guard at all times. Pick-pocketing and bag-snatching can occur, as in any European city, so you should remember the following guidelines:

• Carry as little money and as few credit cards as possible, and leave any valuables in the hotel safe.

• Carry wallets and purses in secure pockets inside your outer clothing, and carry handbags across your body or firmly under your arm.

• Cars should never be left unlocked, and you should remove items of value.

• If your passport is lost or stolen, report it to your holiday representative, Consulate or Embassy at once.

## Currency *see* **Money**

## Customs and Taxes

There is no restriction on the amount of Belgian or foreign currency that can be brought into or taken out of the country.

Personal belongings and clothing intended for your own use are not liable to duty. The duty-free allowance for adults is 200 cigarettes or the equivalent in cigars or tobacco; one bottle of spirits and one bottle of wine, and a reasonable amount of perfume and toilet water.

Hotel and restaurants include VAT and service in their prices. Visitors from non-EU countries who buy an item in Belgium costing more than 7 000BF are entitled to a refund of the VAT (19%) which is included in the price. Ask at the time of purchase for details of how to reclaim this.

## Disabled Visitors

In Britain, RADAR, at 12 City Forum, 250 City Road, London EC1V 8AF ☎ **(020) 7250 3222**, publishes factsheets as well as an annual guide to facilities and accommodation overseas, including Belgium.

The booklet *Batiments accessible aux handicapes en chaise roulante* lists all public buildings, shops, post offices, banks and so on which are accessible to wheelchair-users, and is available from the Belgian Red Cross. This organisation can also give advice to disabled visitors to Belgium on matters such as the hire of aids and equipment. You should write well in advance to Croix Rouge de Belgique, 98 Chaussée de Vleurgat, 1050 Brussels ☎ **00 322 645 44 11** Fax 00 322 640 31 96.

There are special facilities for disabled travellers at some

Belgian railway stations. Enquire in advance to Belgian National Railways, Blackfriars Foundry, 156 Blackfriars Road, London SE1 8EN ☎ **(020) 7593 2332**.

## Driving

Drivers should carry a full national or international driving licence. If you are taking your own car, you should also take insurance documents including a green card (no longer compulsory for EU members but strongly recommended), registration papers for the car and a nationality sticker for the rear of the car.

Your headlights need to be adjusted for driving on the right-hand side of the road. You are required by law to carry a red warning triangle and a first-aid kit. You should also have a spare set of light bulbs.

The roads are well maintained and the free motorway network (no tolls) means you can travel from one end of the country to the other in around 3 hours. The following speed limits apply:

**Motorways** 120kph/75mph
**Major country roads** 90kph/56mph
**Built-up areas** 50kph/31mph

Speeding tickets are issued on the spot and have to be paid within 48 hours.

Remember to drive on the right-hand side of the road. The wearing of seat belts is compulsory in both front and rear seats, and children under 12 must be seated in the rear. Drinking and driving is severely penalised.

It is not really advisable for visitors to drive in the cities – a much better option is to leave your car at your hotel, if there are parking facilities, or to leave it at one of the car parks.

**Bruges** has restrictive traffic policies, there is a strict one-way system and a low speed limit has been introduced to deter traffic congestion. Bruges is very compact, so it is easy to explore on foot or using public transport. If, however, visitors wish to drive to the city, there are several car parks in the south and west of the city (approx. 215BF per day). There is very limited street parking.

**Ghent** also has a complicated one-way system which makes driving difficult, and parking can be a problem. There are car parks in Gouden Leeuwplein near the Belfort, on Sint-Veerleplein near Gravensteen, the Vrijdagmarkt in the north and around the Kouter in the south.

**Antwerp**, unlike most

Flemish cities, does not have such a problem with parking. Pay car parks can be found around the old quayside warehouses along the Scheldt, close to the city centre, and a number of underground car parks (approx. 400/500BF per day). *See also* **Accidents and Breakdowns** and **Emergencies**

### Electric Current
The voltage in Belgium is usually 220V, using a standard two-pin round continental plug, so visitors should bring adapters.

### Embassies *see* **Consulates**

### Emergencies
Police ☎ **101**. The basic accident emergency/ambulance/fire/rescue number is ☎ **100** (there will always be at least one English-speaking operator on call).

### Etiquette
Belgian people are noted for their generous hospitality and the pride that they take as hosts. There are no particular rules of etiquette that are different from those in the UK. Women travelling alone should have few problems, though they should take the usual precautions.

*Vermillion blooms on a traditional guild house balcony, Markt, Bruges.*

Good morning / Goedemorgen
Good afternoon / Goedemiddag
Good evening / Goedenavond
Goodbye / Tot ziens
Today / Vandaag
Yesterday/tomorrow / Gisteren/morgen
Please / Alstublieft
Thank you / Dank u wel
Yes / Ja
No / Neen
How much? / Hoeveel?
Excuse me/sorry / Pardon
Can you help me? / Kunt u mij helpen?
Where are the toilets? / Waar zijn de toiletten?
Do you speak English? / Spreekt u Engels?
I don't understand / Ik begrijp het niet
I'd like … / Ik wil graag …

## Health

Belgium has an excellent health service funded by the State, national insurance and private medical insurance. Under the Reciprocal Health Arrangements, visitors from EU countries are entitled to the same standard of treatment in an emergency as Belgian nationals. To qualify, you should carry an E111 form (available from post offices in Britain). This does not cover all medical expenses, and you are advised to take out health insurance to cover your visit. You will be expected to meet the cost of treatment in the first instance and can claim back 75% of the cost with the E111 form.

Hotels hold a list of doctors and dentists. Pharmacists are used to diagnosing minor complaints and will refer you to a doctor if they feel this is necessary.

## Language

Dutch is the official language of Flanders, with French spoken in Wallonia. You will find that English is widely spoken and understood and you may find menus in both

Dutch and English. While road signs are in Dutch, place names on maps may appear in French or Dutch, which can be confusing to the visitor. For example, Gent (Dutch) is Gand in French, and Ieper (Dutch) is Ypres in French. Opposite are a few words and phrases to help you make the most of your stay.

## Maps

The Michelin Road Map **No 909** Belgium/Luxembourg, which covers the whole country, will help with route-planning and travel between the cities. The *Michelin Green Guide Belgium* includes full information on all the key sights and attractions in the cities, with detailed street plans and background information. The *Michelin Red Guide Benelux* provides details of accommodation and has a list of selected restaurants. The tourist offices also provide maps of Bruges, Antwerp and Ghent.

*Michelin on the Net:*
**www.michelin-travel.com**
Our route-planning service covers all Europe. Options allow you to choose a route and these are updated three times weekly, integrating on-going road-works, etc. The descriptions include distances and travelling times between towns, selected hotels and restaurants.

## Money

The monetary unit of Belgium is the Belgian franc (abbreviated BEF or BF), which comes in 1, 5, 20 and 50 franc coins, and a 50 centime coin (100 centimes = 1 franc). Bank notes are available for 100, 200, 500, 1 000, 2 000 and 10 000BF. Credit cards are widely accepted, the most commonly accepted ones being Visa, American Express, Diners Club and Eurocard. Eurocheques endorsed with a Eurocheque card can be use for sums up to 7 000BF.

Perhaps the safest way to

*Enigmatic Little Gallows House, Groenmarkt, Ghent.*

carry large amounts of money is in travellers' cheques which are widely accepted. Lost or stolen travellers' cheques and credit cards should be reported immediately to the issuing company, with a list of numbers, and the police should also be informed.

Bureaux de change desks are found at the airport and banks. Exchange rates vary, so it pays to shop around. You are advised not to pay hotel bills in foreign currency or with travellers' cheques since the hotel's exchange rate is likely to be higher than that of the bureaux de change.

*See also* **Banks**

## Newspapers

British and foreign newspapers and magazines can be bought in the main cities at newsagents and kiosks, usually the same day. The *International Herald Tribune* and British dailies such as the *Financial Times, Daily Telegraph* and *The Times* are readily available.

The local daily papers are useful for tourists as they include leisure sections, transport timetables, and other relevant practical information.

## Opening Hours

**Shops:** Traditional shop opening hours are 9am-6pm, Mon-Sat. Small shops, bakeries and news-stands can open as early as 7.30/8am. Shops are closed on Sundays, but patisseries and other specialist food shops may open in the morning. Outside the cities, shops may close at noon for an hour or so, in which case they will usually remain open until 7 or 8pm.

**Chemists:** These are generally open 9am-5.30/6pm, Mon-Fri, and Saturday mornings. Lists of chemists which are open late or on Sunday can be found outside each pharmacy.

**Museums:** As a general rule, the large public museums and galleries are open every day except Mondays. Other museums may be open on Mondays but are closed on another day of the week. The Tourist Offices have full details of opening hours for all the attractions within each city.

*See also* **Banks** and **Post Offices**

## Police

If you need assistance, you should approach the *Politie*, who wear dark blue uniforms and usually speak English. A separate national force, the *Rijkswacht*, deals with major crime and polices the motorways; the uniform is a lighter blue, with red trouser stripes.

☎ **101** for the police.

## Post Offices

Post offices are usually open 9am-5pm, Mon-Fri, with smaller branches closing at noon for an hour or two. Some larger ones open on Saturday mornings, but there are no 24-hour post offices in Bruges, Antwerp or Ghent. Stamps are sold in post offices, by newsagents, and in many hotels.

## Public Holidays

New Year's Day: 1 January
Easter Monday: variable
Labour Day: 1 May
Ascension Day: (sixth Thursday after Easter)
Whit Monday: (seventh Monday after Easter)
Festival of the Flemish Community: 11 July
National/Independence Day: 21 July
Assumption Day: 15 August
All Saints' Day: 1 November
Armistice Day: 11 November
Christmas Day: 25 December
Public offices and institutions are also closed on 15

*Waterfront guild houses reflect on their past in tranquil canals, Ghent.*

November (Dynasty Day) and 26 December (Boxing Day).

### Religion

Belgium is predominantly a Roman Catholic country and mass is celebrated in most churches every Sunday. For details of services in other languages, or of churches of other denominations, contact the local tourist board or ask at your hotel.

### Smoking

No smoking signs are easily identifiable and should be obeyed at all times. It is not advisable to smoke in enclosed public places, whether there are signs displayed or not. There are no restrictions outdoors. No-smoking sections in restaurants and bars are rare. Smoking carriages are allocated on all trains, but smoking is not allowed on other forms of public transport, such as trams and buses.

### Telephones

Public telephones take 5BF and 20BF coins, and most will also take phone cards or telecards. Telecards can be bought at tobacconists, newsagents, post offices and public transport ticket offices, for either 200BF or 1000BF. Phones accepting the card can be identified by a telecard sign.

As in most countries, telephone calls made from hotels may be more straightforward and convenient, but they are much more expensive.

Cheap rates apply 8pm-8am, Mon-Sat, and all day Sunday.

For local directory enquiries ☎ **1207** (Dutch), **1307** (French).

For international operator and international directory enquiries ☎ **1204** (Dutch), **1304** (French).

Country codes are as follows:
Australia: ☎ **00 61**
Canada: ☎ **00 1**
Ireland: ☎ **00 353**
New Zealand: ☎ **00 64**
UK: ☎ **00 44**
US: ☎ **00 1**

The country code for Belgium is ☎ **00 32**. The city codes are Brussels (**02**), Antwerp (**03**), Bruges (**050**), Ghent (**09**). If phoning from abroad, delete the **0** in the city code. So, for example, to call Antwerp from the UK, dial **00 32 3** plus subscriber number.

### Time Difference

Flanders is on Central European Standard Time, one hour ahead of Greenwich Mean Time (GMT) in winter and two hours ahead in summer. For most of the year, Flanders is therefore one hour ahead of the time in the UK, five hours ahead of US Eastern Standard, and 14 hours behind Australia (Sydney).

## Tipping

In restaurants, a 16% service charge is usually included in the bill (along with 19% VAT), so you are not expected to tip unless you are exceptionally pleased with the service. You may wish to leave any small change for table service at a bar or café, but this is not essential.

Hotels also include a service charge in the bill so there is no need to tip porters or room service.

It is usual to give a cinema usher a small tip of around 20BF, while in public lavatories there is usually a bowl for you to leave a gratuity (10BF).

## Tourist Information Offices

**Tourist Offices**. It is well worth contacting the Belgian Tourist Office before you go. The international branches cover all the regions and can provide you with basic up-to-date information as well as very useful maps and plans. In London the address of Tourism Flanders-Brussels is 31 Pepper Street, E14 9RW ☎ **0891 887799** fax (0171) 458 0045.

The **Provincial Tourist**

**Offices** are outstandingly efficient and whether you are planning a short or long stay, a visit to the local office is strongly recommended at the first opportunity. They will provide information on tours, hotels, current entertainments, and well-produced glossy brochures with maps. The offices of all three cities publish a free standardised broadsheet guide to gastronomy, shopping and hotels, entitled *Look-out*.

The offices are located at:
**Antwerp:** Grote Markt 15, B 2000 Antwerpen ☎ **(03) 232 01 03**. The Office is on the side of the Grote Markt furthest from the Cathedral.

*Traditional organ music, Bruges.*

**Bruges:** Burg 11, B 8000
Brugge ☎ (050) 44 86 86.
**Ghent:** Predikherenlei 2,
B 9000 Gent ☎ (09) 225 36 41.
The Office occupies the crypt
of the Belfort or Belfry in the
Botermarkt.

## Tours see p.95

## Transport
Each of the three cities has
major underground parking in
the city centre with particularly
easy access from the ring roads
in Bruges and Antwerp
(*see* **Driving**). However, driving
is inconvenient in Antwerp and
Ghent, and virtually impossible
in Bruges.
**Antwerp and Ghent:** Both have
excellent **tram** and **bus** services
(De Lijn company) connected
with the railway stations, and
have flat fares. It is possible to
buy a single ticket from the
driver (40BF) or a ten-journey
ticket (270BF), called a *Rit-
tenkaart*, from news-stands. All
tickets must be 'cancelled' on
boarding the tram, by inserting
into a machine which stamps
the time and date. The ticket
can be used on any other tram
for an hour afterwards. A One
Day Pass allows you to travel on
trains and buses on the urban
network for a day (105BF).
    For **taxies** in Antwerp ☎ 238
38 38; Ghent ☎ 222 22 22/223

23 23/225 25 25.
**Bruges:** Has a good **bus** service
which connects with the
railway station. A One Day Pass
covers unlimited travel on all
city buses (approx. 110BF).
The best way of getting around
the city is on foot or by bicycle.
**Bicycles** can be hired at the
railway station or at Hallestraat
leading out of the Markt (*see
also* **Bicycles**). The city
resounds to the clip-clop of
horses pulling the **open
carriages** that are immensely
popular with tourists. Carriages
can be picked up throughout
the day from the Markt. The
main **taxi** stands are at Markt
(☎ 33 44 44) and Stationsplein
(☎ 38 46 60).

## TV and Radio
BBC long-wave and world
services can easily be picked up
in Flanders, and cable TV
channels are available at many
hotels in the cities. Many
domestic and European
channels also show English-
language programmes.

## Vaccinations
see **Before You Go p.112**

## Water
Tap water is safe to drink in
Belgium, though varieties of
bottled water are available if
preferred.

# INDEX

# INDEX